Green Church

Green Church

REDUCE, REUSE, RECYCLE, REJOICE!

Rebekah Simon-Peter

Abingdon Press
Nashville

GREEN CHURCH
REDUCE, REUSE, RECYCLE, REJOICE!
by Rebekah Simon-Peter

Copyright © 2010 by Abingdon Press

Scripture quotations in this publication, unless otherwise indicated, are from the New Revised Standard Version of the Bible, copyrighted © 1989 by the Division of Christian Education of the National Council of the Churches of Christ in the United States of America, and are used by permission.

This book is printed on recycled paper.

Library of Congress Cataloging-in-Publication Data

Simon-Peter, Rebekah.
  Green church : reduce, reuse, recycle, rejoice! / Rebekah Simon-Peter.
      p.   cm.
Includes bibliographical references.
ISBN 978-1-426-70292-1 (pbk.: alk. paper)
1. Environmentalism—Religious aspects—Christianity.   2. Human ecology—Religious aspects—Christianity.   3. Christian life.   I. Title

BT695.5.S52   2010
261.8'8—dc22

                                                                2009054205

10 11 12 13 14 15 16 17 18 19—10 9 8 7 6 5 4 3 2 1

Manufactured in the United States of America

To the Creator, with loving thanks for trees, rocks, streams, mountains, sky, and the holy mystery of creatures that inhabit them.

Acknowledgments

Writing requires more courage and discipline than I had anticipated, certainly more than I could muster on my own. My heartfelt thanks to those whose names follow; you inspired it in me and demanded it of me. Also, to my readers—Jeanette Baust, Hope Hodnett, Will Morris, Dotty Scott, Mary Ann Tabor, Shantelle Church, and Tabitha Smith—thanks for commas, conversation, and content.

I am grateful also to Rachel Magdalene for providing early course corrections and rigorous standards; to Mary Beth Kiefer for helping to clear away obstacles; to the Honorable Al Gore and the Climate Project for their pioneering work; to Echo Klaproth for the notebook; to my brother Jeff Scott for dangling writing projects in front of me and making it seem possible; and, most especially, to my husband, Jerry Gonzales, whose unstinting support and love make BridgeWorks and writing possible.

Contents

Introduction

These days "going green" is all the rage. Everything from hybrid cars to organic foods, from energy-efficient appliances to recyclable printer cartridges is being touted as green. A recent *USA Today* magazine even headlined an article "Play Green: Your Guide to Earth-friendly Sports." Multinational corporations such as General Electric, DuPont, and Walmart are greening their day-to-day operations. You can now ski green, eat green, and even sleep green—and do it with near religious fervor.

However, what does going green really mean, especially for the person of faith? Is it just about changing types of light bulbs, or is there more to it? Is being earth-friendly just a secular movement or a political agenda, or does environmental stewardship have a place in our life with God?

As it turns out, paying attention to the health of the planet is deeply grounded in the Bible. You could say it is a core biblical value. While the Bible has some 490 references about heaven and 530 about love, it contains over 1,000 references to the earth.

From beginning to end, the Bible is firmly grounded in the wonder and glory of creation. In fact, from Genesis to Revelation, the drama of salvation is played out within the realm of creation. In the beginning, God delights in creating a diverse profusion of life. Even humans come from the humus (soil). "Then the LORD God formed man from the dust of the ground, and breathed into his nostrils the breath of life; and the man became a living

1

being" (Genesis 2:7). In turn, all that God has created delights in the Creator. "Let everything that breathes praise the LORD!" (Psalm 150:6). It is not just those with the breath of life within, though, who praise God. Every aspect of creation sings this chorus of praise. "The heavens are telling the glory of God; / and the firmament proclaims his handiwork" (Psalm 19:1). Even stormy winds and sea monsters join in! (Psalm 148:7-8).

All creation is designed to reflect God's glory and offer praise to the Creator, but sin casts a shadow on the festivities. When sin entered into the garden of Eden, Adam and Eve had to leave. Their responsibility "to till . . . and keep" the garden went unmet (Genesis 2:15), and thorns and thistles cursed the ground (Genesis 3:18). In fact, the creation groans under the weight of sin (Romans 8:22), waiting with eager longing for the children of God to step up to the plate (Romans 8:19). In the meantime, Jesus, incarnation of the Divine, holds all creation together (Colossians 1:17).

Finally, the vision of a new heaven and a new earth is revealed (Revelation 21:1), in which the river of life flows from the throne of God (Revelation 22:1). Abundant fruit trees whose leaves are for the healing of the nations grow on either side of this life-giving river (Revelation 22:2). From Creation to its renewal, nature plays a leading role in the Bible.

Jesus regularly used examples from nature to talk about God. When his disciples worried about God's provision, he urged them instead to "look at the birds of the air" and to "consider the lilies of the field" (Matthew 6:26, 28). Observing nature bolstered their faith as they noticed how God cares for all of creation, including them. When Jesus wanted to teach them about God's universal love, he reminded them to watch the weather: "Your Father in heaven . . . makes his sun rise on the evil and on the good, and sends rain on the righteous and on the unrighteous" (Matthew 5:45). Jesus saw God revealed through nature. And why not? The ancients regularly saw the action and majesty of God reflected in nature. "O LORD, how manifold are your works! / In wisdom you have made them all; / the earth is full of your creatures" (Psalm 104:24).

Consider Psalm 104. While the author was a psalmist, not a scientist, he or she understood and celebrated the interconnectedness of created things:

> You make springs gush forth in the valleys;
>   they flow between the hills,
> giving drink to every wild animal;
>   the wild asses quench their thirst.
> By the streams the birds of the air have their habitation;
>   they sing among the branches.
> From your lofty abode you water the mountains;
>   the earth is satisfied with the fruit of your work.
>
> You cause the grass to grow for the cattle,
>   and plants for people to use,
> to bring forth food from the earth,
>   and wine to gladden the human heart,
> oil to make the face shine,
>   and bread to strengthen the human heart.
> The trees of the LORD are watered abundantly,
>   the cedars of Lebanon that he planted.
> In them the birds build their nests;
>   the stork has its home in the fir trees.
> The high mountains are for the wild goats;
>   the rocks are a refuge for the coneys.   Psalm 104:10-18

Psalm 104 brings to mind that old saying, "A place for everything and everything in its place." The forces of nature are held in balance, and God's wisdom guides them all.

3

Recently, however, we humans have become something of a force of nature ourselves—a destructive force. Through our sheer numbers and patterns of consumption, we are affecting the earth's ecosystems as never before. Jim White, professor of environmental studies and director of the Institute of Arctic and Alpine Research at the University of Colorado at Boulder, and a Christian, spoke at a recent gathering of Christians concerned with the health of creation. Human activity, he said, has had an unmistakable impact on creation. White says that humans have dominated the earth's ecosystems, and our domination has affected the planet's basic functioning.

The National Council of Churches has noted symptoms of earth's degradation in a February 2005 open letter to church and society called "God's Earth Is Sacred":

> God's creation delivers unsettling news. Earth's climate is warming to dangerous levels; 90 percent of the world's fisheries have been depleted; coastal development and pollution are causing a sharp decline in ocean health; shrinking habitat threatens to extinguish thousands of species; over 95 percent of the contiguous United States forests have been lost; and almost half of the population in the United States lives in areas that do not meet national air quality standards. . . . We have become un-Creators. Earth is in jeopardy at our hands.

Unfortunately, unlike the animated film *WALL-E*, we cannot just move to another planet while robots clean up and restore this one. In fact, as persons of faith, we are enjoined by Scripture to exercise responsibility for the health of the planet. That is exactly what this book is designed to help you do.

Individual action is good, and much has been written about it; but this book aims for something more. The truth is that changing light bulbs, while a good start, simply is not enough to restore balance to the creation. We must work in concert—group by group, congregation by congregation, community by community, and nation by nation to restore the creation. After all, the Bible calls us to communal action in the matter of stewardship. We must work together on a large scale.

This book, then, aims to help you think and act communally for the good of God's creation. While many of us have exchanged our incandescent light bulbs for compact fluorescent light bulbs at home, and maybe even at church, we have not thought about the far-reaching impact our churches can have on the health of the planet. This book will help you do so.

The book begins with the theme of repentance and how we have sinned against the creation. We then move on to reclaim our role as stewards of God's good creation. Next, we move into the heart of going green by looking at how to apply the concepts of reduce, reuse, and recycle to our communal life of faith. Finally, we will rejoice in God's promises to us and our role as co-creators with God.

Going green is a life-long adventure, one that is grounded in biblical commands, stories, principles, and values. While it may start with simply changing light bulbs, perhaps you will find that it even changes the way you look at life, faith, the church, and God.

Whatever this book accomplishes in you, I pray that it will renew your relationship with Jesus Christ, "the firstborn of all creation." For as the writer of Colossians tells us, Jesus is at the very heart of creation. "In him all things in heaven and on earth were created . . . and in him all things hold together" (Colossians 1:15, 17).

For his sake, let the adventure begin!

1. Repent

God saw everything that he had made,
and indeed, it was very good.
Genesis 1:31

We have forgotten who we are.
Now the land is barren
And the waters are poisoned
And the air is polluted.
United Nations Environmental Sabbath Program

The Days of Creation

The story of Creation in Genesis thrills me. I love its majesty and intimacy. On the one hand, God called forth the entire creation through the spoken word. On the other hand, God surveyed it with delighted satisfaction and called it good. In simple but elegant poetry, Genesis 1:1–2:3 describes what the psalmist celebrated: "The earth is the LORD's and all that is in it, / the world, and those who live in it" (Psalm 24:1).

The word *genesis*, in Hebrew and Greek, means "beginnings." *Beginnings* refers not only to its placement in the Bible but the beginnings of heaven and earth itself. Even more important, Genesis describes the primary relationship between Creator and creation.

We can see that most especially in the first week of Creation. Over the course of six days, God created the entire natural world including humankind. It is a diverse but interdependent web of life.

On the first day, God created light and separated day from night. Interestingly, this was not the kind of light given off by sun, moon, or stars. They were not even created until several days later. This light is the very presence of God that makes all life possible.[1] "God said, 'Let there be light'; and there was light. And God saw that the light was good" (Genesis 1:3-4a).

On the second day, God separated the waters above from the waters below by creating the sky. "God said, 'Let there be a dome in the midst of the waters, and let it separate the waters from the waters'" (Genesis 1:6). In the ancient Near East worldview, this sky (or dome or "firmament") was thought to be a solid element that held the rains back from flooding the earth. It was of particular importance because water was the ancient symbol of primeval chaos, the very enemy of order. Mastery over water belonged to the Divine. In fact, Genesis opens with the image of "the spirit of God . . . hovering over the waters"[2] (Genesis 1:2, New International Version). The King James Version emphasizes the immensity of this chaos by pointing out that "darkness was upon the face of the deep" (Genesis 1:2). If light equals life, then this chaos was a state deeply devoid of life or order; but God's creative speech tamed and transformed the chaos.

On the third day, God separated dry ground from the gathered seas. The land then produced seed-bearing plants and fruit-bearing trees. "God said, 'Let the waters under the sky be gathered together into one place, and let the dry land appear'" (Genesis 1:9). Having separated the waters above from the waters below and containing the chaotic seas, God then called forth a wild profusion of trees, flowers, grasses, fruits, and vegetables. The dark, deep, watery chaos was transformed into a verdant scene bursting with self-replicating life. "And God saw that it was good" (Genesis 1:12).

On the fourth day, God sparkled the heavens with the sun, moon, and stars. Here is light that we can relate to. These luminaries not only give light and separate the day from the night, but they act as "signs to mark seasons and days and years" (Genesis

 **Question**

What Would God Say Now?

In the beginning, God saw everything that he had made, and indeed it was good; but what would God say now? Suppose God asked you to rate the health of creation today. Consider what you know about the air, atmosphere, precipitation, forests, oceans, streams, vegetation, fish, birds, air, wildlife, and human communities. How would you rate the health of creation on a scale of one to five?

5 Perfect health; as pristine and unpolluted as the garden of Eden
4 Some wear and tear but functioning as God created it to function
3 Rough at the edges; feeling the strain of nearly 7 billion people
2 Dangerously polluted, overpopulated, and impoverished
1 Desperate shape; barely surviving as in the days of the Flood

1:14, NIV). God's artistry was growing increasingly beautiful, increasingly complex. "And God saw that it was good" (Genesis 1:18).

On the fifth day, God caused the seas to swell and swim with oceanic life and the skies to fill with the winged songs of birds. "Let the waters bring forth swarms of living creatures, and let birds fly above the earth across the dome of the sky" (Genesis 1:20). The self-replicating nature of creation expanded. It was not just vegetation that reproduced, but fish and birds as well.

This was a fertile world indeed, one that was meant to produce and reproduce—life abundant! "Be fruitful and multiply," God commanded the fish, "and fill the waters in the seas, and let birds multiply on the earth" (Genesis 1:22); and "God saw that it was good" (Genesis 1:21), just as we do.

On the first part of the sixth day, God spoke and filled the land with animals. " 'Let the earth bring forth living creatures of every kind: cattle and creeping things and wild animals of the earth of every kind.' And it was so" (Genesis 1:24). Throughout these six days of Creation, God spoke into being a wondrous web of life. Out of chaos, God created light and dark, day and night, sky and earth, precipitation and flowing waters, seas and land, plants and trees, seeds and fruit, fish and birds, sun and moon and stars, daily and seasonal rhythms, and animals and their young. All of it was punctuated by the joyous refrain: "And God saw that it was good" (Genesis 1:12, 18, 21, 25).

However, the creation was not proclaimed "very good" until God created humans. In an act of divine delegation, God created male and female in God's own image. Then God blessed and directed them with these commands: "Be fruitful and multiply, and fill the earth and subdue it; and have dominion over the fish of the sea and over the birds of the air and over every living thing that moves upon the earth" (Genesis 1:28). We are co-creators with God; we are to rule over this harmonious order for the good of all creation.

The fruitfulness of creation was complete and so was God's joy: "God saw everything that he had made, and indeed, it was very good" (Genesis 1:31). One can imagine God's vibrant delight and satisfaction with this beauteous, harmonious, self-replicating creation.

Finally, on the seventh day, a number signifying wholeness and completion, God rested. Like an artist satisfied that a masterpiece is complete, God blessed and hallowed the day. All was well.

The Grief of God

Some five chapters later, however, the scene is radically different. God was in despair. Like a lover betrayed, the Creator had become disillusioned with the creation. It was not the trees or fish or sky causing problems, though; it was humanity. Adam and Eve had disobeyed God and eaten of the Tree of Knowledge of Good and Evil. God cast them out of the garden of Eden with just the clothes on their backs. Later jealousy and murder entered the scene when Cain killed his brother Abel. Strife, ego, and pride were not far behind.

By Chapter 6 of Genesis, God is fed up. The earth was filled with violence, and every inclination of the human heart was evil. God was grieved to have made us at all! So with a pained heart, God made a drastic decision: to be done with humanity and, by default, with the rest of creation. Human beings are so intimately interconnected with the rest of creation that we cannot exist apart from each other. The health and wholeness of one depends upon the integrity of the other. Humans had sinned not only against God but against the creation. As a result, the creation itself was corrupted.

In a terrifying move, God set about unmaking what had been made and allowed the created order to revert to chaos. Water, God's opponent, was let loose. For forty days and forty nights, God caused it to rain. It was a non-stop, torrential deluge of water: a flood such as the earth had never seen before. However, before putting an end to it all, God made a covenant with the one person who still had integrity: Noah. "Noah was a righteous man, blameless in his generation; Noah walked with God" (Genesis 6:9).

11

God instructed him to build a large boat of cypress wood that would survive the coming chaos. "But I will establish my covenant with you," God said to Noah, "and you shall come into the ark, you, your sons, your wife, and your sons' wives with you. And of every living thing, of all flesh, you shall bring two of every kind into the ark, to keep them alive with you; they shall be male and female" (Genesis 6:18-19). Then God shut them in the ark that Noah had built and proceeded to decreate.

The Process of De-creation

Remember that on the first day God created light and separated day from night. In the midst of this deluge, though, day and night became practically indistinguishable. Light was blotted out. While the moon, sun, and stars had not stopped shining, there was so much rain that the light could hardly be seen. Light as a precursor to life was gone as well. Without light, the interdependent web of life started to unravel.

On the second day, God tamed chaos by creating sky, separating the waters above it from the waters beneath it. However, in this nonstop torrent, the sky all but disappeared. "On that day all the springs of the great deep burst forth" from beneath and the "floodgates of the heavens" above were "opened" (Genesis 7:11, NIV). With water flowing from every direction, the horizon between sky and earth was effectively erased.

God separated the land from the seas so that dry ground might appear and vegetation grow on the third day. However, the Flood submerged everything—from the lowest valleys to the highest peaks. Not one blade of grass was visible. Not one tree-top broke through the water. Not one mountain crest pierced the seas. For 150 days, earth itself was submerged. In fact, it would be more than a year after the Flood began that dry land would reappear. Chaos was returning.

On the fourth day, God created the sun, moon, and stars to guide the seasons; but even the seasons were undone in that year of de-creation. There was no longer any distinction between "seedtime and harvest, / cold and heat, / summer and winter" (Genesis 8:22, NIV). It was just one waterlogged day after

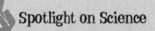 **Spotlight on Science**

Figuring Environmental Impact
Impact = Population x Affluence x Technology

This simple equation has been proposed as a way of estimating human impact on the environment through phenomena such as global warming, deforestation, and species loss. The greater the population, the more affluent it is; and the greater the technology involved, the higher the impact. Forty years ago, when the equation was pioneered, technology was seen as a detriment. Today, that may not be true. Technology is so much a part of our lives that it is almost impossible to factor it out. In fact, used wisely, new technology may help us reduce our overall impact on the environment.

another in this time of submersion and survival. Without seasons, the ordering of life was disrupted.

Remember the fifth and sixth days? That was when God filled the waters with living creatures, the skies with great winged birds, and the land with animals and human beings. Practically all that biodiversity was wiped out by the Flood. With no place to nest and no vegetation to eat, even birds will have died off. Perhaps the fish survived, but even they would have been affected by the absence of light.

All but eight humans and the pairs of reproducing creatures were drowned. The web of life was in tatters. God's artistry was unmade. Chaos had won.

God Repented

After 150 days, though, something astonishing happened. God repented. God turned from de-creation to reconciliation. Just as in the beginning, when "a wind from God swept over the face of the waters" (Genesis 1:2), God made a "wind blow over the earth" (Genesis 8:1) so that the waters subsided. "Never again!" God declared within his heart. "Never again will I destroy all living creatures, as I have done" (Genesis 8:21, NIV).

Later God established a covenant with Noah, his descendants, and "every living creature" with him: "Never again will all life be cut off by the waters of a flood; never again will there be a flood to destroy the earth" (Genesis 9:11, NIV). The rainbow is God's sign to all creation of this eternal promise; and the rainbow is with us still, a sign that God's covenant with creation is still in operation.

Tragically, while God's promises to us have been kept, humans are now doing the very things God repented of. After the Flood, God reaffirmed the goodness of creation—in spite of human sin—and reestablished order over chaos; but chaos is reasserting itself. The trees, fish, and sky are not causing problems; humanity is, for we are unmaking and de-creating what God called good. As the National Council of Churches letter to church and society declares, "We have become un-Creators."[3]

Ecological Meltdown

Un-Creators? This is a strong word, especially for those of us who love God with all our hearts, minds, and souls, and our neighbors as ourselves. However, the evidence shows that through our sheer numbers and unsustainable ways of living, human beings are now overriding the delicate balances of the natural world.

When the words of Genesis were committed to parchment, perhaps 50 million people filled the earth. Now, nearly 7 billion people fill the earth.[4] By 2050, it is estimated that more than nine billion people will fill the earth.[5] Yes, we have been fruitful and multiplied and filled the earth—so much so that some scientists think we have reached the earth's carrying capacity. The earth, they say, simply cannot sustain this many people without her systems crashing. Surely the poor among us will suffer the most.

Signs of this are already evident. Not only is our fruitfulness harming the earth that sustains us; but many of us simply do not have enough water, food, shelter, clothing, or work to sustain meaningful lives. "About half [of the world's population] live in poverty and at least one fifth are severely undernourished. The rest live out their lives in comparative comfort and health."[6]

If more than 50 percent of us battle for enough, the rest of us face another problem: over-consumption. Not only do we face obesity, we are depleting the earth's limited natural resources. As we consume, we leave behind an increasingly polluted planet in our wake. According to the Union of Concerned Scientists, water and air pollution are two of the four most damaging consequences of over-consumption.[7] One look at the trash that now washes up on beaches—including plastic bags, plastic bottles, tires, and fast-food containers—is dark affirmation of this. The oceans have become our dumping grounds.

The human population is growing exponentially and with it our ecological "footprint" on the earth. We continue to cultivate land on which to grow food, build homes, extract minerals, manufacture products, construct stores, and multiply cities. The impact on the rest of God's creation is like an ecological "Twilight Zone."

"Life itself is vanishing," reports the Species Alliance. "All over the world, animal and plant species are disappearing at an unprecedented and alarming rate."[8] This is not the Rapture; this is the largest mass extinction since the age of the dinosaurs. Biologists predict that fully half of all species on earth may be gone within the next 50 to 100 years.[9]

These numbers leave us in shock. Disappearing species include one quarter of all mammals and one in eight birds.[10] In addition, bees, which pollinate one third of all crops and are integral to our way of life, are dying off. One third of bee colonies in the United States and the United Kingdom have collapsed, even as the collapse is spreading to other countries.[11] At the same time, bat colonies in the Northeast United States are experiencing a similar decline due to "white nose syndrome." Voracious predators, bats are integral to healthy ecosystems since they eat insects, moths, and beetles.[12]

Phytoplankton, a microscopic species at the bottom of the ocean's food chain, is feeling the heat from global warming. While healthy marine life—including krill, fish, and whales—depend upon healthy phytoplankton, their populations are declining with global warming.[13]

God said to Noah about the animals he was rescuing, "Keep them alive" (Genesis 6:20). Under our watch, however, the earth's bio-diversity is vanishing. God commanded Noah to save species; we seem to be throwing them out of the ark.

Our over-consumption seems to have another grave effect: global warming. Carbon dioxide is one of the main contributors to global warming; and as of 2002, 40 percent of US carbon dioxide emissions come from burning fossil fuels. This gas traps heat in the earth's atmosphere, causing the earth's temperature to rise.[14]

While pockets of debate still linger on the role of human-caused global warming, the majority of scientists agree. The Intergovernmental Panel on Climate Change (IPCC), an international group of leading scientists, evaluates all the research done on global warming. In its 2007 report, the IPCC said it is more than 90 percent certain that human activity is causing global warming.[15] Their "view has been supported by

Green Fact

Where's the Beef?

To reduce your impact on the planet, consider eating vegetarian meals at least one day a week. Figure 13.5 pounds reduction of carbon dioxide per person per week. If ten people eat vegetarian meals one day a week for the remaining five weeks of the study, that adds up to 13.5 x 10 x 5 for a total of 675 pounds less carbon dioxide in the group's carbon footprint. That is the equivalent of driving 675 fewer miles during the study. If everyone in your church committed to this, you could reduce your carbon footprint by a great deal. To get the ball rolling, cook up a "green" church potluck with beans, grains, pasta, vegetables, fruits, and nuts. Serve it on real dishes, and eat it with real silverware! Bring your own dishes and silverware to lessen the clean-up time. Enjoy the tastes and the company.

the world's leading senior scientists, including the majority of living Nobel Prize winners in the sciences."[16] Even scientist Wallace S. Broecker, who coined the term *global warming* but is not entirely convinced of human contributions to it, warns, "We dare not sit back and do nothing . . . [while we] wait for more information."[17]

The earth's temperature has already risen "an average of 0.5 to 1.1 degrees Fahrenheit" over the last 100 years.[18] That does not seem like much. In fact, you may live in a part of the world where that change would be welcome. Yet, one degree of warming is already wreaking havoc. Major Antarctic ice sheets are breaking up,[19] 90 percent of the world's largest glaciers are melting,[20] and ocean levels are rising appreciably. As ocean levels rise, coast lines are affected. At least one Inuit village along the Alaskan coast has already relocated.[21] New sand is being hauled in to rebuild Florida beaches as ocean levels rise.[22] As frozen expanses melt, waters are being let loose. Are we seeing a return of the primeval chaos?

If we continue burning fossil fuels at our current rate, scientists foresee a potential rise of six degrees Celsius in the next century.[23] *National Geographic* advises that "six degrees could change the world."[24] The impact would range from an ice-free Arctic to a dried-up Amazon rainforest to submerged coastal cities.[25] These changes would devastate life on earth.

Our Need to Repent

God has delegated divine authority to us. We are co-creators who may rule and have dominion over the earth for the good of all creation. Yet the earth is crying out to us through polluted air and water, profuse trash, mass extinctions, extreme weather, and changing landscapes. Meanwhile more than half of the world's humanity is desperate for the basic stuff of life. What has gone wrong? It seems that we who have been called to care for creation have become sinners against the creation.

It is time to repent.

I do not write these words easily. For a long time, I have tried to run from this knowledge. It seemed too big and overwhelming to cope with. When I first learned about many of these problems, I was an environmental studies major at the University of Vermont. Back then, some twenty-five years ago, much of this breakdown had not yet occurred; it was still projected into the future. *Someone will do something about this,* I thought, *before it's too late.*

Two years ago, I had an epiphany: That "someone" is me. And you. Based on that realization, I decided with my husband to buy an energy-efficient hybrid vehicle. We have stepped up our recycling efforts, changed out our incandescent light bulbs to the ones that look like soft-serve ice cream cones (compact fluorescent bulbs), said no to paper and plastic bags and become friends with canvas bags. We buy 100 percent recycled paper. We have purchased energy-efficient appliances, winterized our house, and turn off lights when not in use. I teach community classes and speak to church and interfaith groups. I let my elected officials know what I think. Overall, my husband and I have raised our awareness and reduced our carbon and ecological footprints.

Perhaps you do all these things and more. If so, you may have had the same sneaking suspicion as I did: It is not enough. We need a worldwide movement that recognizes the creation as sacred and our responsibility to it as divinely commanded. As persons of faith, we need to stand together for God's good creation before it is too late to hold the chaos back.

Many congregations have remained silent on environmental stewardship because it has been so politicized. I wonder, though, if we can afford the luxury of ambivalence. I believe the price is too high. A close reading of the Scripture reveals that the health of the creation is a moral, spiritual, and religious issue. It is one that deeply concerns the people of God.

For those who are not convinced that global warming is caused or affected by humans, consider cutting back on carbon emissions to help reduce dependence on foreign oil and resources. In other words, if you do not believe this is an environmental issue, perhaps you can think of it as a national security issue. Whatever your political position may be, surely we can agree and work together on the care of God's creation.

The time for us to act is now. Scientists used to advise that we had eight to ten years to make significant changes in the way we live before some of the climactic changes underway are irreversible. Now we may be at the tipping point. The window of opportunity is small, but it is enough time for us to repent. After all, God repented of de-creation in forty days. Can we follow suit?

The good news is that because human beings are responsible for the care of creation, there is a possibility that we can repair and restore it. However, we cannot do it without God's help. Together, let us turn back to God and repent of our disordering, disruption, and de-creating of all that God has called good. God will grant us courage and guidance.

There have been voices crying in the wilderness for decades, centuries even, about the failing health of the creation. Now many people are waking up to the reality that the health of God's creation is our responsibility. Persons of faith are joining forces to green their congregations and communities. It gives me hope—for us and for future generations. Thank you for deciding to be part of this extraordinary effort.

Faith Without Works

"Faith without works is dead" (James 2:20, King James Version). In the same way, repentance without action is meaningless. You can begin now to restore the creation by greening your house of worship. Start by becoming aware of the level of creation consciousness at your church. As noted in the introduction, the Bible is grounded in the wonder and glory of creation. Creation even plays a leading role in the drama of salvation; but what kind of role does it play in the life of your church?

To answer this question, start by looking at your services of worship, since worship is at the heart of a church. Consider in what ways awareness of the creation is present in your congregation's worship life. Look at worship bulletins from the past month. Do you notice any hymns, songs, prayer concerns, prayers, psalms, Scripture readings, testimonies, sermon themes, litanies, anthems, children's sermons, or even announcements that highlight the creation and our relationship to it?

The next time you are in worship, look at the worship space itself. Are there banners, paraments, wall hangings, or stained-glass windows that highlight the creation? Does your sanctuary incorporate any elements of creation, such as natural sunlight, large windows, majestic views, or natural building materials? Take notes so that you can discuss your findings later. On a scale of 1 to 5, how would you rate your congregation's awareness of its relationship to creation?

Follow Up

Share what you have learned with family members, your group, your pastor, and others in your church. Discuss the urgency and benefits of making changes. Make positive suggestions about how God's good creation might play a bigger role in your worship life.

2. Reclaim

Then God said, "Let us make humankind in our image,
according to our likeness; and let them have dominion over
the fish of the sea, and over the birds of the air, and over the
cattle, and over all the wild animals of the earth, and over
every creeping thing that creeps upon the earth."

Genesis 1:26

In Chapter 1, we saw that God repented from destroying creation and calls us to do the same. By reclaiming our rightful relationship with creation, we put feet on repentance. In this chapter, we will explore our God-given role as stewards of creation as well as discover how to reclaim it.

Stewardship

In the early 1970's—the decade that gave us the first Earth Day, the establishment of the US Environmental Protection Agency, the oil embargo with long lines at the gas pump, the Clean Water Act, the first national air-quality standards, and a ban on lead-based paints—I turned ten. That is when I found a green ecology poster folded up at the bottom of a box of tissues. I carefully extracted it, taped it to my closet door, and was hit with a sudden conviction: I am going to save the earth! In psychological circles that is called a Messiah complex; in theological circles it may well be called stewardship.

Stewardship is the wise and careful management of some-one else's resources. In ancient times, a steward might manage the household, money, possessions, servants, or affairs of state for another. Although we do not use the word much today, think property manager, portfolio manager, butler, or nanny, and you get the idea. Stewards are entrusted with something valuable, sometimes priceless, that belongs to another.

Stewardship is also a deeply biblical idea, although I did not know it at the time of my childhood epiphany. The psalmist said, "When I look at your heavens, the work of your fingers, / the moon and the stars that you have established; / what are human beings that you are mindful of them, / mortals that you care for them?" (Psalm 8:3-4). The answer follows: As God is mindful of us, so we are to be mindful toward God's handi-work—if not to save it, at least to steward it. "You put us in charge of your handcrafted world, / repeated to us your Genesis-charge"[1] (Psalm 8:6, *The Message*).

So what exactly is the Genesis-charge? Accurate decipher-ing of this term has been the center of controversy and debate. To uncover its meaning, let us go back to the middle of Day 6 of Creation and see for ourselves.

The Crown of Creation

During the first five and a half days of Creation, God was hard at work. Step by step, God created the conditions for life. First, God separated one element from another—the waters above from the waters below, and the dry land from gathered seas—to reveal sky, oceans, and earth. With these three realms established, God called on them to produce the creatures that would inhabit them. "Then God said, 'Let the earth put forth vegetation'"

(Genesis 1:11) and "let the waters bring forth swarms of living creatures, and let birds fly above the earth" (Genesis 1:20).

With these realms now populated, we arrive at the middle of Day 6. God is about to create humans. Drumroll, please! This is a pivotal moment in the Creation story, not just because it is us that we are talking about but because the text indicates something different is about to unfold. "Then God said, 'Let us make humankind in our image, according to our likeness'" (Genesis 1:26).

Rather than the habitat itself giving rise to a new inhabitant, our template is divine. We alone are patterned after the Creator's own self. While the rest of creation bears the fingerprints of God, we bear the very stamp of God. Made in the image and likeness of God, humans are the crown of creation. That is not to say that humans are not part of creation; we are. The Hebrew word for "humankind" is *adam*, from which we derive the proper noun *Adam*. In Genesis 1:26, however, when God proposed to make us, the word was not yet used as a proper noun. Instead, it was a description of the kind of creature God intended to create.

To the hearers of this ancient story, which was transmitted orally long before it was written down, *adam* sounded like *adamah*, "ground." While the New Revised Standard Version translates *adam* as "humanity," a more descriptive translation might be "earth creature." Our connection to the earth is as deeply imprinted within us as our connection to God—maybe even more so, for in the second Creation story of Genesis the connection is made explicit: "Then the LORD God formed man [*adam*] from the dust of the ground [*adamah*], and breathed into his nostrils the breath of life; and the man became a living being" (Genesis 2:7).

On the one hand, we are part of the created order. We exist within the mutual fabric of creation that God spoke into being—not just in theory but in practice. The creation supplied Adam and Eve with food (Genesis 1:29; 2:16), pleasure (Genesis 2:9), wisdom (Genesis 3:5-7), clothing (Genesis 3:7, 21), livelihood (Genesis 3:17-19), and encounters with God (3:8). Human well-being is utterly dependent on the good workings of the whole creation.

 Question

What Do You Believe Is Our Purpose?

a. Humanity is the grand finale of creation; the rest of creation exists solely for our purpose and use.

b. Our purpose is to dominate the rest of creation and keep it in line.

c. Our purpose is to peacefully coexist with the rest of creation.

d. Our purpose is to conserve and preserve the rest of creation.

e. Other

That is as true today as it was then. For example, have you ever tried to make lunch without drawing upon the bounty of the earth? It cannot be done. Even if you are having a plastic sandwich, neon chips, and a diet pop from the corner store, your lunch still finds its source in the earth. There is no life for humanity without a healthy creation.

On the other hand, humans are set apart from the rest of creation. Just as God made "the greater light to rule the day and the lesser light to rule the night" (Genesis 1:16), so humans are to rule over earthly habitats and their inhabitants. This, then, is the "Genesis-charge": "Let them have dominion over the fish of the sea, and over the birds of the air, and over the cattle, and

26

over all the wild animals of the earth, and over every creeping thing that creeps upon the earth" (Genesis 1:26). This charge is no small purpose; and it bears great responsibility, similar to becoming a parent or a caretaker. Humans are now set into the footprints and concerns of the Divine.

How to interpret these verses has generated considerable controversy and debate and has led to different understandings of our relationship to the earth.

Deconstructing Dominion

For many people, the word *dominion* brings to mind the idea of domination and control. The earth is ours to do with as we please. Nature exists solely for our purposes; we may change, manipulate, or destroy whatever we want for the sake of humankind. Who cares about the rest of creation? It is here to serve us. We are more significant than the birds, fish, animals, or vegetation.

Once upon a time, when the earth was lightly populated, this may have made sense. As population growth has exploded, however, some scientists believe this faulty interpretation of dominion has been singularly responsible for the environmental crises that we face today. That may well be true. If so, we need to deconstruct that understanding of dominion and reconstruct one that is life-giving and biblical.

To do so, we need only look at the Creation story again in which *dominion* appears. In Genesis 1, the Creator is life-giving, sharing generative powers with the rest of creation. Vegetation produced seed, trees produced fruit, birds produced nestlings, and fish and land animals had offspring. Every creature was granted the innate ability to self-replicate, each according to its own kind.

We humans get in on that deal, too, when we have offspring; but here is where God's creativity is extravagantly generous. Not only do we reproduce according to our own kind, but we are in a sense mini-reproductions of the Creator as well—not in identity, of course, for that privilege belongs to Christ alone (Colossians 1:19) but rather in relationship to the creation.

Extending the royalty metaphor found in Genesis, humans are like vice-regents entrusted with oversight of the earthly domain. According to Hussein Amery, associate professor at Colorado School of Mines, this same theme is found in the Qu'ran, making it common to Judaism, Christianity, and Islam.[2] What a timely way to build bridges of understanding across religious lines. As royal representatives of God, people of many faith traditions are called to mirror God's self back to the creation. Together, we are all called to be caretakers of the earth.

What exactly is it that we are to mirror? The answer lies within the biblical image of God portrayed thus far. Consider how the Divine King is portrayed in Genesis 1. This is no power-seeking dictator or self-serving tyrant. Rather, this is an inventive, creative, generous, and benevolent sovereign. This ruler labors on behalf of the royal subjects and regards each one with delight, calling them good.

Our dominion is to follow suit. Our sacred task and divine purpose is to extend that kind of generous rule over all the royal subjects in God's domain. We are to continue God's creative work of making space for, blessing, and sustaining the fish of the sea, the birds of the air, the cattle, all the wild animals of the earth, and every creeping thing that creeps upon the earth (Genesis 1:26). In other words, we honor the image and likeness of God by maintaining the goodness, wholeness, and integrity of all that God has created, not by destroying it.

Original Blessing

After creating humans, God spoke. In keeping with the generous nature of the Creator, these first words are sanctifying: "God blessed them" (Genesis 1:28). The theme of this blessing, however, is not about our relation to the Divine, but to the earth itself. "Be fruitful and multiply, and fill the earth" (Genesis 1:28). This is a blessing of abundance.

Here comes the sticking point, however. What is a blessing for us sounds like a burden for the rest of creation. Not only are we to be fruitful and fill the earth, we are to "subdue it" (Genesis 1:28). The word *subdue* has generated as much controversy and debate as *dominion*. *Subdue* seems to imply an enemy to overcome and defeat; but according to biblical scholar Terrence Fretheim, there is no enemy in sight here. We are part and parcel of this creation. To defeat the creation would be to defeat ourselves.[3] Rather than suppress or oppress the creation, *subdue* has a deeper meaning that is in keeping with the character of a benevolent God. The word would be better understood to refer to the process of tilling and cultivating the land.

Bringing land into food production required hard work, especially in the days before modern tools. However, it was not necessarily a violent undertaking nor did it destroy the creation. On this scale and setting, agriculture would have enhanced the soil, maintained biodiversity, and provided food. Later, God commanded the Israelites to leave some harvest in the field to be gleaned by the poor, the widows, the orphans, and the aliens (Leviticus 23:22; Deuteronomy 24:21).

God's blessing on humanity is meant to bless all of creation. The interconnected network of life will sustain humans, while we in turn will steward it so that all life may flourish. This meaning of *subdue* is made all the more clear by another blessing. Read what God said to the fish and the birds the day before humans were made: "God blessed them, saying, 'Be fruitful and multiply and fill the waters in the seas, and let birds multiply on the earth.' And there was evening and there was morning, the fifth day" (Genesis 1:22-23).

Sound familiar? It is almost word for word what God said to the first humans. We are to be fruitful and multiply in order to fill the earth; fish and birds are to do the same in the waters and the skies, respectively. While we may be the crown of creation, we are not the whole of it. Creation is blessed before us and without us. The wondrous web of life God spoke into being is sacred in its own right. The original blessing God granted to fish and birds is no less binding or important than ours. If humans, fish, and birds are each called to flourish in our respective habitats, how can we do it in such a way that we do not cancel out each others' blessings?

Creation Out of Balance

As stewards of creation, according to Genesis 1, we are to balance the blessings bestowed on fish, birds, and us while bringing the land into agricultural production. We are to work with the earth in such a way that it sustains us all. However, that is not what is happening. Human population and technology have reached such a state that the way we live is changing and depleting all the domains of creation: air, water, and land. So what do we do?

Balancing blessings does not mean we need to kill off human beings to reduce population. (Our unbalanced way of living may accomplish that on its own.) However, it does mean we come to terms with the facts and get a picture of the way things are, so that we might once again act in the best interests of all creation.

As Jesus drew lessons from nature, let us also "look at the birds of the air" (Matthew 6:26). I can hear their chirping from

Spotlight on Science

Global Weirding

Since the Industrial Revolution of the late nineteenth century, the earth's atmosphere has been heating up.[4] According to NASA's Goddard Institute for Space Studies, most of the jump in average temperatures since 1895 (1.3 degree Farenheit) has come in recent decades. In fact, the last two decades of the twentieth century were the hottest in 400 years and possibly the warmest for several millennia.[5] It is not just the air that has been getting warmer; the earth's oceans have been warming as well.

This dramatic shift in our earth's environment is what is known as climate change or global warming. Thomas Friedman, author of *Hot, Flat, and Crowded: Why We Need a Green Revolution and How It Can Renew America*, calls the shift "global weirding."[6]

What is weird? How about daffodils that bloom in January?[7] or April Cherry-Blossom Festivals that now take place in March?[8] or West Nile virus spreading across North America?[9] or Glacier National Park's 150 glaciers melting away to 27 in the last century?[10] or colorful coral reefs bleached white?[11] or a staggering increase in the frequency and intensity of wildfires, tornadoes, floods, drought, heat waves, and tropical storms?[12]

my study as I write this, but things are changing for the birds. Once common birds are disappearing, including familiar sparrows, the common grackle, the common tern, and the Eastern meadowlark. According to an Audubon Society study, the top 20 species have declined on average by an alarming 68 percent.[13] Writer and farmer Verlyn Klinkenborg suggests the Audubon report says more about us than about birds: "We are the only species on earth capable of an ethical awareness of other species and, thus, the only species capable of happily ignoring that awareness. . . . I don't suppose that most Americans would actively kill a whippoorwill if they had the chance. Yet in the past 40 years its number has dropped by 1.6 million. In our everyday economic behavior, we seem determined to discover whether we can live alone on earth."[14]

Can you imagine a life without birds? That is what is beginning to happen. Consider the baby bird. As temperatures rise and the length and timing of seasons shift due to climate change, baby birds are caught in the crunch. For example, robins arrive in my part of the country on average two weeks earlier in the spring than they used to. The worms and other foods they feed their hatchlings, however, do not.[15] No wonder the bird songs we grew up with are being silenced.

However, it is not just birds that are being squeezed or warmed out of existence. Count fish in that number, too. We are overfishing the oceans to the point of collapse. Much of that is due to high-tech fishing operations, such as huge floating fish-processing factories, trawlers the size of football fields, and dragging operations' nets that scrape the ocean floor, not to mention mismanagement, greed, and overconsumption.[16] We do not need all these fish to feed the world's population. According to writer Fen Montaigne, "an incalculable number of fish" are caught by trawlers and suffocated in the process. These dead fish are thrown out and never eaten.[17]

Meanwhile sharks, swordfish, tuna, and marlin have all but disappeared from the world's oceans.[18] Globally, only ten percent of these fish remain in the world's oceans. Additional fish in the same boat, so to speak, include haddock, sea bass, hake, red snapper, orange roughy, grouper, grenadier, sturgeon, plaice, rockfish, and skate. All this is happening while the world's population is exploding. We are "committing ecological

♺ Spotlight on Science

What Is Causing Climate Change?

Many scientists believe that at the heart of climate change are human activities—namely, deforestation and the burning of fossil fuels such as coal, oil, gasoline, and natural gas. Burning these fuels produces carbon dioxide (CO_2). When CO_2 enters the atmosphere, it thickens it, trapping more of the sun's radiation inside the atmosphere. This "greenhouse effect" is similar to covering up with a blanket or two on a chilly night; it keeps the heat in. While the greenhouse effect is a natural process, it has been greatly amplified by an increase in human-generated CO_2. Unfortunately, we cannot just kick off the covers when the atmosphere gets too warm.

The earth has natural cycles of warming and cooling. What we are experiencing now, however, is far outside the normal range of natural variability. By looking at the chemical structure of the CO_2 molecules in our atmosphere, climate scientists can trace the higher levels of CO_2 directly back to emissions from cars and trucks, power plants, manufacturing, and burning of forests. According to NASA, the level of CO_2 in the atmosphere is now higher than at any time in the last 650,000 years.[19] Before the Industrial Revolution, it had never risen above 300 parts per million.[20] By the year 2050, as population increases, it is projected to hit 600 parts per million.[21] Neither we nor the creation were designed to live under such circumstances.

and economic suicide."[22]

Families in the eastern Canadian province of Newfoundland can attest to this. There, cod fishing had been a way of life for centuries. In 1992, fishermen went out to sea to catch cod, just as they always had. That year, the fish never appeared. For years, high-tech fishing factories had harvested schools of fish faster than they could reproduce. Finally, the cod simply were not there. Forty thousand people lost their jobs. Many more were plunged into poverty. The impact was felt by small and large fishing operations alike.[23]

This scenario is being played out all over the world. A *National Geographic* report says, "Scientists predict that if we continue fishing at the current rate, the planet will run out of seafood by 2048 with catastrophic consequences."[24] Bye-bye lobster dinners, frozen fish sticks, and jobs.

Eighty percent of our planet's biodiversity is underwater.[25] Oceans are home to an amazing array of wildlife, much of which has yet to be catalogued and much of which will be lost if we continue to foul our waters. It is time to sound the global alarm!

Reclaiming Stewardship

Sounding the alarm means a radical change in the way we live and the way we see ourselves. The Bible calls us to be stewards of the creation, but most of us are content to be mere consumers. That is especially true of us in the industrialized West. If it is there, we want it. Whether or not we can afford it or need it, clever marketing tries to convince us to buy it. Once we get it, we rarely pay attention to the long-term impact of our wants, especially on those in poorer countries who have been forced off their land by multinational agribusinesses and must seek a new life in urban slums.

I cannot help but wonder what would happen if the Consumer Price Index, a popular indicator of the health of the economy, were re-invented as the Stewardship Price Index. An index such as this could reveal the health of our economy, the health of the planet's underlying ecology, and the health of the poor. By pinpointing the human and ecological costs of our choices in dollars and cents, we might see the real price tag of our lifestyles.

Economy and ecology are deeply connected in more than one way; they are related to the word *steward*. The words *economy*

Green Fact

CFLs

The word *incandescent* means "to glow with heat,"[26] and that is exactly what incandescent lightbulbs do. Ninety percent of their energy is turned into heat; only ten percent is turned into light. Compact fluorescent light bulbs (CFLs), on the other hand, convert energy into about 75 percent light and about 25 percent heat; and they last ten times as long.[27] Using CFLs instead of incandescent light bulbs in rooms where lights are on for at least four hours per day will save 100 pounds of CO_2 annually per bulb.[28] Put incandescent bulbs in places where lights are on less than fifteen minutes at a time. Too much flipping of switches makes them burn out much faster (although that may change as technology advances).

---

and *ecology* derive from the Greek *oikos*, or "house," for which a steward, *oikonomos*, is the manager.[29] To be a good steward is to manage carefully all the resources in one's care.

There is something else I wonder: *Is it too late for us to make a difference and learn to live together in fruitful harmony? Or can we find a way to live into our biblical call?* I look around at the world, and I honestly wonder.

However, as Christians we live by hope, so the answer must be yes. It is not a blithe yes, though, for in order for it to be fulfilled, this yes must be grounded in the Scriptures, sounded out by science, enacted in faith, and lived out in our daily lives. Fortunately, no one is better situated to do this than communities of faith. We have the moral backing. We have the theological framework. We have the organization. We have multigenerational memory to ground us. We have future generations to consider. I am not saying it will be easy. Likely it will not be. However, God's creation is worth our best efforts.

Reclaiming Nature

I have the privilege of being a Big Sister in the Big Brothers Big Sisters program. Two years ago, my husband and I took my then-12-year-old Little Sister Tabitha camping. It was her first time in a tent or in the woods—ever. We had a blast! We hiked through the meadows, listened to the coyotes yip, watched the sun set, and gazed upward at the twinkling heavens. Finally, we ate s'mores while telling ghost stories around the campfire.

Tabitha enjoyed it all. What intrigued her most, however, was a pond swollen by snowmelt and the activity of beavers. She wanted to get in that water. She edged around it for a while. Finally, she hopped onto an old square fence post, launched into the pond, and played sailor for a while. Then she lost her balance and slipped into the water. She was soaking wet, with water dripping from her hair, sneakers, t-shirt, and shorts; but she had a huge smile on her face. Tabitha was having the time of her life.

"Sorry," she said half-heartedly, expecting to get into trouble. I was not sorry, not at all. I was thrilled that she had had the experience. Some children swim with dolphins; Tabitha swam with the beavers, literally. Like many young people, she had spent much of her time plugged in to headphones, a cell phone, video games, and television. She could recite movies by heart, but she did not know a spruce from a pine or a woodpecker from a hummingbird.

The truth is, we will not be able to reclaim our role as stewards of the environment if we never spend any time out in it. Young people will not grow up caring about the creation if they do not have direct experiences in it, and that type of experience is becoming increasingly rare. Richard Louv, author of *Last Child in the Woods*, writes, "In the United States, children are spending less time playing outdoors—or in any unstructured way. From 1997 to 2003, there was a decline of 50 percent in the proportion of children nine to twelve who spent time in such outside activities as hiking, walking, fishing, beach play, and gardening."[30] Louv calls this condition "Nature Deficit Disorder."[31]

His unofficial diagnosis "describes the human costs of alienation from nature," including "diminished use of the senses, attention difficulties, and higher rates of physical and emotional illnesses."[32] Louv affirms that the disorder "can be detected in individuals, families, and communities."[33] I think it can be found in churches, too.

Christian education used to be grounded in camp experiences where the holy met the wild. Not anymore. The move indoors has affected faith formation, too. For economic reasons churches are selling off their camps at record rates due in large part to underuse and underfunding. That means fewer children have the chance to sing the Psalms outdoors, sit around the campfire and tell their stories, or let Christ speak to them through the whistling wind in the pines. They are more likely to spend the summer at basketball camp or computer camp than they are playing outdoors. Not surprisingly, the number of young people who hunt, fish, or participate in 4-H or camp with their families are down, too—never mind playing in the backyard or down by the creek.

Americans still love nature; but for most of us, our relationship to it has become iconic. We digitize it into screensavers. We Photoshop it and forward it in e-mails. We view it safely from a distance on the Discovery Channel, or we zoom over it on four-wheelers. However, we spend decreasing amounts of time actually wandering around in it, observing it, and watching it. We have become, in a word, de-natured; and that is taking a toll on us and on the creation. We are more depressed, more anxious, and fatter. Likewise the creation is going through a series of crises we cannot see or imagine.

It is not just children who spend less time in nature. Adults are spending less time with the creation as well. A few months ago, my doctor told me I had a vitamin D deficiency, which came from a lack of exposure to the sun. A vitamin D deficiency? I could not believe it. I grew up walking back and forth to school, playing in the woods behind my house, ice skating, skiing, and horseback riding.

As an environmental studies major, with an emphasis on botany, I spent much of my college career exploring the Green Mountains of Vermont and the Cloud Forests of Costa Rica and serving as a volunteer naturalist. After college, I was an acid rain researcher, collecting samples from lakes and ponds in the Vermont countryside. I was always outside.

It was hard for me to understand how I could have a vitamin D deficiency. However, I had to admit it had been a long, cold, windy winter in Wyoming; and even though it is ill-advised to diagnose oneself by reading books, it came to me as I read *Last Child in the Woods* that I had more than a vitamin D deficiency: I had nature deficit disorder, and I had it bad. Somehow, in the last few years, I had traded in green time for screen time; and it showed. I was going stir crazy.

My husband, a Wyoming native, is fond of saying that when he grew up, his mom would tell him and his six brothers and sisters, "Go outside, and don't come back 'til dark!" If a parent did that today, Jerry jokes, they could be brought up on charges of child neglect. Yet those are the experiences that imbued so many of us with our initial love of nature.

I think it is time for all of us to get back out into the creation, to be restored and reclaimed, and to reclaim our rightful role as stewards of the creation. So plant a garden. Take a walk. Swim with the beavers. Take a child outside. Exult in the creation. While you are out there, pay attention. Listen. Watch. Breathe deeply. Read the Bible outdoors. Pray for the creation. Let the Spirit speak to you about how you might use your God-given talents to bring order out of chaos in your neck of the woods.

And don't come back 'til dark!

The Church Building

Global climate change is one of the most pressing symptoms of our inadequate stewardship of creation. Conservation is a first step in the right direction and is also good stewardship of your congregation's money. This week, survey your church building to see how you can make it more energy-efficient. Consider the following:

♻ Energy-efficient lighting, such as CFLs instead of incandescent bulbs, and the use of motion-sensitive lights in bathrooms, hallways, and entryways. Where is daylight sufficient without the use of additional lights?

♻ Energy-efficient heating and cooling systems, electronics, and kitchen appliances. Look for the Energy Star logo.

♻ Energy efficiencies such as on-demand water heaters or an insulation jacket on the furnace.

♻ Use of alternative energy sources such as solar panels on the roof, passive solar design, or wind-powered electricity.

♻ Water-conservation measures such as low-flow toilets and faucets that do not leak or drip.

♻ A bike rack in the parking lot.

♻ Easy access to public transportation or a van to pick up riders.

♻ Grounds that are landscaped appropriate to the climate. For example, are you trying to grow cactus in Seattle or lush greenery in the desert?

♻ Receptacles for trash. Are your grounds littered with wind-blown plastic bags or other trash? Do you have enough receptacles to encourage proper disposal of garbage and recyclables?

Follow Up

Using the notes you took, speak to the pastor or trustees about what surfaced during your informal energy-efficiency survey of the church. Thank them for their hard work. Then offer positive suggestions on how your congregation can better exercise stewardship of the creation through conservation. You might even lend a hand.

3. Reduce

Thus the heavens and the earth were finished, and all their multitude. And on the seventh day God finished the work that he had done, and he rested on the seventh day from all the work that he had done. So God blessed the seventh day and hallowed it, because on it God rested from all the work that he had done in creation.

Genesis 2:1-3

Busy, busy, busy seems to be the default setting these days. When I go the grocery store, it is not uncommon to be greeted, "How're you doing? Staying busy?" as if busy is the ideal life. While it may not be ideal, it is definitely the new norm. However, nonstop busyness is not good for us; and it is killing the creation. As we think about reducing our impact on the earth, there is no better place to turn than to the Bible for guidance. It contains the first environmentally friendly law on the books, the covenant of sabbath.

God Rested

In the beginning, God created the heavens and the earth. For six days God ordered chaos and brought forth beauty. Finally, the work of creation was complete. "Thus the heavens and the earth were finished, and all their multitude" (Genesis 2:1). At that point, God did not just start anther project, as many of us might. Instead, God "rested on the seventh day from all the work that he had done" (Genesis 2:2). The word *rest*, sometimes translated "cease," comes from the Hebrew *shabbat*, from which we get the English word *sabbath*.[1] Just as each of the previous six days contained specific acts, so God's intentional act of ceasing creating on the seventh day is significant; sabbath now becomes part of the created order.

"So God blessed the seventh day" (Genesis 2:3). Up until this point, God had blessed only creatures: fish, birds, and humans, each with a special commission of bounty and abundance. However, God then blessed a period of time "and hallowed it because on it God rested from all the work that he had done in creation" (Genesis 2:3). *To hallow* means "to make holy" or "to consecrate as sacred."[2] The sacred commission of the seventh day is to be a holy oasis in time in honor of the creation and the Creator.

Sabbath's gift is the freedom to be and to be like God. As vice-regents of God, stewards of the creation, mini-reproductions of the Creator, we too are invited to rest, to cease creating, to be finished with what we are doing. In fact, not only are we invited to, we are commanded to.

The sabbath commandment is the fourth of the Ten Commandments[3] and appears in Exodus 20 and Deuteronomy 5. It is referenced extensively throughout the rest of the Bible as well. In the fourth commandment, we are called to observe a day of rest every seventh day. I find it interesting that while the other days of Creation occur just once, the seventh day, or sabbath, is repeated weekly. Our rest recreates God's rest and thereby honors the majesty and magnificence of creation. This "perpetual covenant" (Exodus 31:16) is "given in order that you may know that I, the LORD, sanctify you" (Exodus 31:13).

Mother's Day, Father's Day, Christmas, and birthdays come once a year. No matter how much you may enjoy these holidays and the people they honor, the cycle of observance is annual. It is interesting, then, that one day per week is set aside to honor and commemorate the creation as a gift of the Creator. That elevates creation to a high level.

God commanded, "Remember the sabbath day, and keep it holy" (Exodus 20:8). In Hebrew, holiness implies separation or distinction. Think back to the six days of Creation. Just as night is separated or distinguished from day, the waters above are separated or distinguished from the waters beneath, and the seas are gathered together so that dry land might appear, so the seventh day itself is set apart from the preceding six. It is a day destined or hallowed for different activities than the previous six.

While the first six days of the week were given over to inventive productivity, the seventh day marks completion. This is not the kind of completion that necessarily means everything is checked off the to-do list; it simply means we decide to take a break, whether we are finished or not.

A friend once told me that if I could not say no to a request, then I could not say yes either. All my yeses were not choices; they were simply knee-jerk reactions to other people's requests. In the same way, if we cannot choose to abstain from work or to refrain from busyness, then all of life is one unending to-do list. Is that the purpose of our lives? Not according to the fourth commandment.

"Six days you shall labor and do all your work. But the seventh day is a sabbath to the LORD your God; you shall not do any work" (Exodus 20:9-10). On the seventh day we may say no without guilt, remorse, or pangs of conscience. That goes for everyone in the family, from the head of the house to its lowliest members. Who works on the sabbath? "Neither you, nor your son or daughter, nor your manservant or your maidservant, nor your animals, nor the alien within your gates" (Exodus 20:10, NIV). Even animals get a day off, not to mention children, servants, and visiting workers.

"For in six days the LORD made heaven and earth, the sea, and all that is in them, but rested the seventh day; therefore the LORD blessed the sabbath day and consecrated it" (Exodus 20:11). While the fourth commandment does not say what you should do on the sabbath day, it definitely says what you should not do: work and labor.

Observing the Sabbath

Jews and Christians have been observing sabbath for centuries now, but how we have marked this special day of rest from work has changed over the years. In Jesus' time, Jews went to synagogue on that day to read and discuss the Scriptures.[4] Naturally, Jesus (Luke 4:16) and Paul (Acts 17:1-2) did likewise. Along with the rest of the Jewish community, the disciples kept the sabbath (Luke 6:1-5) as well. In fact, Jesus made much of his observance of the sabbath; it was the topic of many discussions.[5]

After the Resurrection, the early church celebrated the sabbath on the seventh day of the week (Saturday)[6] and the Lord's Day on the first day of the week (Sunday). Over time those two became conflated, and the sabbath was transposed to the Lord's Day. Now almost all Christians celebrate the Lord's Day as the sabbath.[7]

That is certainly how it was when Connie and Carlyle were growing up. Lifelong Methodists now in their nineties, this married couple grew up in a time when dancing, playing cards, and going to the movies were forbidden on Sunday. Instead, Sunday was spent worshiping, eating family meals, and being involved in quiet play.

My family's observance of sabbath was quite different. I was raised Jewish in a family of seven by my Jewish mother and Catholic father. Our family's religious observances took on the feel of interfaith experiments. We ate matzoh at Passover and ham at Easter, and we celebrated Christmas and Chanukah.

For a while, we had big Sunday dinners like my father had eaten growing up. Then we made Friday night, the Jewish sabbath,

Question

Is Sabbath Part of Your Life?

Sabbath is an ancient concept that denotes rest. It is time made holy by not working. Is sabbath part of your life?

Choose the answer that best fits your own sabbath practice.

a. I take sabbath time every week. Time apart is important.
b. I take some down time now and then.
c. Vacations are my sabbath.
d. Sabbath is overrated. I like staying busy.
e. Who has time to rest? I will sleep when I die!

our family time. On that night, we would have a special *shabbat* dinner served on the good dishes in the dining room instead of the kitchen. Dinner would begin with my mom lighting two slender white candles over which she pronounced the Hebrew blessing that welcomed in the sabbath. Then my dad would bless the wine in his pretty good pretend Hebrew. Finally, after a third blessing of thanksgiving over bread, we would tear into the delicious *challah*—a loaf of braided egg bread sprinkled with poppy seeds. Then came the meal itself, always something special. After dinner, we would scatter and go our separate ways, sometimes to temple, sometimes not. With that, sabbath was over for us.

As I grew older, I first rebelled against my religious upbringing and then came to embrace it more deeply. TGIF (Thank God It's Friday), once a call to party, became a sweet sigh of anticipation for that sacred oasis in time. In the little Jewish community of Montpelier, Vermont, my home after college, Jews of every affiliation were embraced in our small synagogue. It was there that I realized the sabbath was intended to encompass a full twenty-four hours. So, for the first time ever, from Friday sunset to Saturday sunset, I practiced the sabbath disciplines of traditional Jewish communities: not working, not handling money, and not driving. I say "practice" because it took discipline to give up the patterns of the larger world I lived in. Being part of a practicing Jewish community made it easier, though.

In that community I came to find that the seemingly restrictive "thou shalt nots" of sabbath made room for expansive "thou shalts." Thou shalt enjoy thy life! Just do it without spending money. Thou shalt relax! Just do it without getting in the car or driving anywhere. Thou shalt enjoy nature! Just do it without taking from it. It is a clever setup, really. As with reality television shows that give you a budget of $250 to remake a room or $15 to feed a family of four, it was the restrictions that inspired creativity.

While sabbath can be interpreted as restriction, Deuteronomy 5 envisions sabbath in the opposite way: freedom from restriction. "Remember that you were a slave in the land of Egypt, and the LORD your God brought you out from there with a mighty hand and an outstretched arm" (Deuteronomy 5:15). When the Israelites were enslaved, God's power proved greater than all the pharaohs of Egypt. "Therefore the LORD your God commanded you to keep the sabbath day" (Deuteronomy 5:15).

Sabbath is God's gift of freedom from injustice and from enslavement to work.

I find it interesting that God offers sabbath as a living testimony to freedom from unjust labor, yet so many of us want to reenslave ourselves to work—as if work could save us instead of the mighty hand and outstretched arm of the Lord. I count myself in that number. As I look at the calendar, I realize I am writing this chapter on the sabbath day. The day of rest that God has given me, I have given back. Thanks but no thanks, God; I have work to do.

"On it, you shall not do any work," the text insistently reminds me. Interestingly, though, one translator renders that passage, "You are not to make any kind of work."[8] I surely know how to make work. Just ask my husband. Every new project I take on makes work for him, and vice versa.

Our projects also make work for the planet. Take the simple act of driving, so much a part of daily life in the United States. Driving our cars, whether Hummer or hybrid, means a labor-intensive, energy-intensive, and dangerous enterprise of getting petroleum out of the ground, refining it, transporting it, and selling it. I live close to the Sinclair Oil Refinery in Wyoming. Recently, an accident there dumped 2,730,000 gallons of gasoline into the ground. Another accident released large quantities of hydrogen sulfide, a potentially fatal gas, into the atmosphere.[9]

Thankfully, no one died in either case; but the incidents were not without cost to the air, soil, and groundwater. The costs to human health, birds, and wildlife are not yet known. Doubtless, the effects will be long-term. The ways we live and drive make work for the planet. However, sabbath helps level the playing field. It makes rest for everyone. It also makes rest for the planet.

One weekend, when I still lived in Montpelier, my older brother Jamie drove up from Connecticut to visit me. On Saturday afternoon, he and I walked about four miles up a dirt road lined by maple trees that arched gracefully overhead. We visited the whole way up and back. If it had not been for sabbath, we probably would have sandwiched in a hurried ten minutes on the phone. More likely, we would not have talked at all. As I look back on it, that sabbath was a day of honoring the creation. By not working, handling money, or driving, I reduced my workload, time pressures, and acquisitiveness, all of which allowed me to breathe a sigh of relief. It also reduced my carbon footprint, allowing the earth to breathe a sigh of relief, too.

Sabbath, Science, and Sustainability

Jonathan Ormes, retired NASA scientist, and I made plans to meet while I was on my way to lead a women's retreat on the topic of sabbath and the environment. I wanted to talk with him about my theory that practicing sabbath is an environmentally friendly discipline.

"Absolutely," he said. "In fact, we can tell from space where and when people are observing the sabbath all around the world."

"Really?" I asked, "from space?" This was better than I thought.

He said, "We can see that levels of nitrous oxides—byproducts of fossil-fuel combustion, among other things—fluctuate during the week. They go down on Friday in Islamic countries; down on Saturday in Israel; and down on Sunday in the United States, Europe, and Japan. Those levels don't go down at all in China; the numbers stay pretty steady throughout the week. This lowering of nitrous oxide levels is called the sabbath effect or the weekend effect."[10] In other words, the less people drive and the less industry produces, the cleaner the air.

Listening to Dr. Ormes, I marveled at the convergence of science and spirituality. The Scriptures call us to be stewards of the creation; science lets us know how we are doing at it. According to Dr. Ormes, not too well. For the elevated presence of nitrous oxides during the week is connected to ozone smog and acid rain, which are dramatically changing the atmospheric composition.[11]

Perhaps it is no coincidence that the intended outcome of sabbath observance—being refreshed(Exodus 23:12; 31:17)—can also be translated as "paused-for-breath."[12] Childhood asthma is on the increase, as are other respiratory difficulties. All are linked to the quality of our air.[13] Sabbath rest literally clears the air and gives us breathing room. In fact, sabbath reveals itself as the first environmentally friendly biblical covenant. Sabbath is good for people and the earth. It is not a stretch to say that faith grounded in the Bible is "green." Sustainability is built into the very fabric of creation.

That is one of the reasons Christopher Ringwald, author of *A Day Apart: How Jews, Christians, and Muslims Find Faith, Freedom, and Joy on the Sabbath*, invites us all to step back from our normal activities one day a week. The environmental boon from observing the fourth commandment, he notes, would be significant. He calculates that by remembering the sabbath and keeping it holy, we could cut our impact on the earth by over 14 percent. Imagine if we were to keep all three sabbaths![14]

The Sabbatical Year

Did you know that three sabbaths are outlined in the Bible? Each one is designed to reduce our impact on the rest of creation. Each one is also calibrated to the number seven, the symbolic number of wholeness or completion. While the weekly sabbath takes place every seven days, a sabbatical year takes place every seven years; and a year of Jubilee takes place after

Spotlight on Science

The Weekend Effect

Weekends are different from weekdays in more ways than one. Not only are they designed for rest, but the earth can tell when we are refraining from work. NASA scientists have detected a "weekend effect." They can tell from space where in the world sabbath is being observed on Friday, Saturday, or Sunday because air pollution rates go down in regular, observable ways.

However, this phenomena is not just visible from space; we can see it on the ground. There is some evidence that weather changes depending on the day of the week. In the southeastern United States, based on the amount of particulate matter in the atmosphere, especially from commuting, the frequency and severity of rainstorms and lightning has been linked to the day of the week.

Using satellite data, scientist Tom Bell at NASA's Goddard Space Flight Center linked pollution levels with weather patterns to discover that in that part of the country, rainfall tends to increase in frequency during the week and decrease on the weekend. This appears to be due to heavier midweek particulates in the air from commuting.[15] Storm development and lightning strikes also seem to follow this pattern.[16] In other words, weather patterns tend to follow our work patterns, at least in one part of the United States. So if you want better weather on the weekends, try honoring the sabbath. Leave the car in the garage!

seven cycles of sabbatical years.

While the sabbath day provides rest for the household, the sabbatical year provides rest for the land. "Six years you shall sow your field, and six years you shall prune your vineyard, and gather in their yield; but in the seventh year there shall be a sabbath of complete rest for the land, a sabbath for the LORD" (Leviticus 25:3-4a).

If the weekly sabbath day takes discipline and a leap of faith, imagine the trust required for the sabbatical year, in which "you shall not sow your field or prune your vineyard" (Leviticus 25:4). As those who work the land know, it is not wise to plant the same thing over and over on the same piece of land. Planting in this way depletes the soil.

Much like our own need for rest, farmland has to lie fallow so it can later produce. Even so, during biblical times when the sabbatical year was practiced, people still had to eat. To do so they had to trust in volunteer crops: "You may eat what the land yields during its sabbath" (Leviticus 25:6). The bounty that resulted was meant for the entire community: "You, your male and female slaves, your hired and your bound laborers who live with you; for your livestock also, and for the wild animals in your land all its yield shall be for food" (Leviticus 25:6-7).

Keep in mind there were no convenience stores, grocery stores, or a system of refrigeration to turn to. In an agricultural society dependent on growing its own food, the sabbatical year meant unsurpassed levels of faith in soil, God, and neighbor. This yield had to get them through the sabbatical year as well as the following year when crops would once again be planted.

However, sabbath is about more than trust; it is also about justice. Exodus 23 reframes the sabbatical year and the sabbath day as acts of justice for the most vulnerable: work animals, slaves, aliens, and the poor. "For six years you shall sow your land and gather in its yield; but the seventh year you shall let it rest and lie fallow, so that the poor of your people may eat; and what they leave the wild animals may eat. You shall do the same with your vineyard, and with your olive orchard. Six days you shall do your work, but on the seventh day you shall rest, so that your ox and your donkey may have relief, and your homeborn slave and the resident alien may be refreshed" (Exodus 23:10-12). The sabbatical year affirms that all of creation—especially the poor, the vulnerable, and the voiceless—has the right to be treated with dignity and compassion.

The Jubilee Year

The third type of sabbath, embodied in Jubilee, furthers the ideals of justice. This additional year of rest occurred every seven cycles of sabbatical years. "You shall count off seven weeks of years, seven times seven years, so that the period of seven weeks of years gives forty-nine years" (Leviticus 25:8).

In Jewish tradition, Jubilee was to begin on Yom Kippur, the day of repentance, with the blast of the shofar, the ram's horn. "Then you shall have the trumpet sounded loud; on the tenth day of the seventh month—on the day of atonement— you shall have the trumpet sounded throughout all your land" (Leviticus 25:9). As the sabbath day is consecrated to a special purpose, the Jubilee year is sacred, hallowed. "And you shall hallow the fiftieth year and you shall proclaim liberty through- out the land to all its inhabitants" (Leviticus 25:10). It is thought that Jubilee is "the year of the Lord's favor" referred to by Jesus in Luke 4:19.

Jubilee begins in atonement and repentance and ends in the returning of land to its ancestral owner. "In the year of jubilee the field shall return to the one from whom it was bought, whose holding the land is" (Leviticus 27:24).

Like the sabbatical year, Jubilee provided rest for the land. Even more, though, Jubilee provided humans with "rest" from acquisition and greed. During this time, each family was to relinquish newly acquired property and return to their ancestral lands: "In this year of jubilee you shall return, every one of you, to your property" (Leviticus 25:13).

Fair trade was built into the Jubilee economy, and the sale of land was to be calculated by the number of harvests available until the next Jubilee. "When you make a sale to your neighbor or buy from your neighbor, you shall not cheat one another. When you buy from your neighbor, you shall pay only for the number of years since the jubilee; the seller shall charge you only for the remaining crop years" (Leviticus 25:14-15). At the deepest level, Jubilee reminds us that the earth is not private property. "The land must not be sold permanently, because the land is mine and you are but aliens and my tenants" (Leviticus 25:23, NIV). No matter how much money changes hands, ownership remains with the Creator. Do you hear echoes of Genesis here? We are stewards of the land, not its owners.

In a recent speech, Bishop Elaine Stanovsky said, "I learned a new word recently: *philopatry*. It means love of homeland. It describes what fish and birds and animals do when they return to their nesting grounds year after year to bring forth new life." There is a connection to Jubilee here. The word *jubilee* is a rough transcription of the Hebrew word *yovel*, sometimes translated as "homebringing," because it was time to bring oneself and one's possessions back home.[17] "It shall be a jubilee for you: you shall return, every one of you, to your property and every one of you to your family" (Leviticus 25:10b). Just as the fish of the sea, birds of the air, and animals of the land love their homes and return year after year to nest and give life to the next generation, and as the Jewish people of biblical times loved their ancestral homes, so too we love ours.

I look out my window at the Uplift, a low ridge of undeveloped mountains that runs through the center of town, which comforts me every time I return home from my travels. I gaze at the flowers in the garden that lift their friendly faces toward the sun. I look up at the one blue sky that covers all the earth, and I long for my home to remain the same. However, I fear that the innate philopatry that brings us home for Jubilee celebrations will not be possible for future generations, or maybe even for our own. The landscape around us changes daily, succumbing to unceasing human pressures.

I recently returned to Parker, a suburb of Denver, where I pastored a decade earlier. Nothing looked familiar. The fields and wetlands were covered with high-end shopping centers. The last of the ranches had been converted to strip malls. All the open space was covered with buildings. I felt so disoriented and saddened, I was not even sure I was in the right city. Imagine, then, how the native birds, ducks, geese, beavers, fox, rabbits, wolves, coyotes, lynx, bobcat, deer, elk, moose, and bear feel when there is no place for them to come home to. No wonder an increasing number of wild animals are found wandering into cities. It is time for a new Jubilee for all God's creatures.

Revisiting Sabbath

Sabbath is a lovely concept: six days on, one day off; six years on, one year off; every fifty years the forgiveness of debts and the return of ancestral properties. But how realistic is it? Most people do not lament the disappearance of blue laws that legislated Sunday as a day of rest by prohibiting commerce. Many people have jobs that require them to work weekends. We are so mobile that the idea of leaving work behind has become anathema.

We are so busy that what remains of sabbath for most us is more of a nod toward the holy than a full-immersion experience. Like the Friday night dinners of my youth, many Christians get just a taste of what sabbath offers. We may attend Sunday morning worship, relax over an extended brunch, get out on the golf course, or spend time in the garden. After a few hours, though, it is right back to the default setting: busy, busy, busy. Some families do not even get that much time off as children's sports programs or the need to work two or three jobs steadily encroaches upon the last remaining chance at rest. Yet as noted biblical scholar Walter Brueggmann observes, "A life that cannot imitate the creator in rest is in the end self-destructive . . . . Such a life . . . in the end violates the very fabric of creation."[18]

So, what might sabbath look like in the post-modern world? I believe the words of Jesus may hold the key. He asked, "Is it lawful to do good or to do harm on the sabbath, to save life or to kill?" (Mark 3:4). According to Jewish law and practice, although one does not work in honor of the sabbath, saving a life on that day is and always was permitted. What if we take Jesus' words to heart by doing good for creation on the sabbath? The life we save may be our own!

One way to begin is by observing an environmental sabbath. First established by the United Nations Environment Programme (UNEP), this is a time for faith communities to observe a day of rest for the earth. Many beautiful prayers written for this occasion can be found in *Earth Prayers From Around the World: 365 Prayers, Poems, and Invocations for Honoring the Earth*. Praying for the health of the earth is a great way to expand our concern to include all of creation. Lifting up the sabbath as an ecological covenant may encourage your congregation to bring about a renewed interest in the creation.

From there, you might consider incorporating a newly designed event, "Season of Creation," into your church's worship or liturgical calendar. Beginning in September, the event lasts four weeks and celebrates with Christ the wonders of creation.

 **Green Fact**

A Sabbath From Driving

Every gallon of gas used generates approximately twenty pounds of CO_2.[19] If you chose not to drive one day per week, fifty-two weeks per year, that could save over half a ton of CO_2. Imagine if everyone in your church decided to take a sabbath from driving once a week. Depending on the size of your church, you could prevent 26–5,200 tons of CO_2 from entering the atmosphere.* Now imagine if every church in your community signed on. Wow! The earth would surely breathe a sigh of relief.

Churches of 50 would save 26 tons of CO_2
Churches of 100 would save 52 tons of CO_2
Churches of 500 would save 260 tons of CO_2
Churches of 1,000 would save 520 tons of CO_2
Churches of 2,500 would save 1,300 tons of CO_2
Churches of 5,000 would save 2,600 tons of CO_2
Churches of 10,000 would save 5,200 tons of CO_2

*Based on 25 miles of driving per day at 25 miles per gallon.

According to the program's designers, "in the seasons of Advent, Epiphany, Lent and Easter we celebrate the life of Christ. In the season of Pentecost we celebrate the Holy Spirit. Now, in the season of Creation, we have an opportunity to celebrate God, the Creator."[20]

Just as many churches observe a "carbon fast" at Lent, at which time they reduce their carbon footprint over the course of forty days, you and your church group might try a "low-carbon sabbath." Perhaps you will choose to refrain from driving on that day or choose not to turn on your television, computer, or other electronic devices. Perhaps you will choose to walk or carpool to church. Maybe you will choose to refrain from spending money or shopping for that one day a week. If doing this for an entire day seems too hard, start by taking a specified amount of time off from work to "remember the works of the LORD"[21] (Psalm 77:11, New King James Version).

One summer, the church I served had Sunday morning services and Sunday evening services. During those long summer days, I spent the time between services on the couch. I read for spiritual refreshment. More often than not, though, I simply gazed out the living room window at Elk Mountain. I did no other work for profit or pleasure. For the first time in many years, I was practicing sabbath again. Unfortunately, I had left behind that oasis in time some years earlier when I exited the Orthodox Jewish community to enter into Christian discipleship. It felt good to reimmerse myself in a mini-sabbath. I think my parishioners sensed something was different, too. Actually, it was not hard to miss. I came back to church relaxed and rejoicing instead of tired and grumpy.

Mini-sabbaths such as these are a great way to remember the sabbath and honor its intentions. Be deliberate in setting aside time for your mini-sabbaths. Write them on your calendar, and treat them as true commitments. Light a candle, say a prayer, turn off the television, and turn off the phone. Go outside into nature, if possible. Let the sun play on your face, feel the breeze in your hair, and let God speak to your soul. Bless the creation. Rest, relax, and let the "weekend effect" take effect in you.

"But I don't work," you may be saying. "I'm retired." Yet retired persons are some of the busiest people among us. "I don't know how I ever found the time to work," a recently retired parishioner confided in me. "I'm doing more now than ever before!" News flash: Keeping busy is just another form of work. So here is my challenge to you: Take a day off from volunteering, mentoring, staffing the soup kitchen, running errands for your neighbor, or being a pillar of your family and community. Even God "rested and was refreshed" (Exodus 31:17). Even if you do not need the break, the creation does.

Which day should you observe sabbath? Some Christians are adopting the practice of the early church by honoring the creation on the seventh day of the week, Saturday, and the Lord's resurrection on the first day of the week, Sunday. Others reclaim the dual emphases of creation and Christ together on Sunday. Another option is to carve out mini-sabbaths at another time during the week. It may not matter as much which day you set apart as how you start to synchronize your life with the rhythms of creation so that healing may begin.

Sabbath is important for reducing our stress and our impact on the planet, but do not make it impossible to experience sabbath. If you cannot start with a day of rest, how about an hour? Then month by month expand that hour until you have reached a full day of rest. I invite you to try it. You just might like it. I will be right alongside you.

Turn It Off!

Does your church equipment take a sabbath? Turning off equipment when it is not in use reduces cost, energy consumption, and global-warming pollution. Check to see if the following are turned off after use:

- ♻ lights
- ♻ computers
- ♻ printers
- ♻ routers
- ♻ copy machines
- ♻ fax machines
- ♻ televisions, DVD players, and other classroom equipment
- ♻ sound and video equipment in the sanctuary

Many electronics draw power even when turned off, especially those with black transformer boxes, so you might want to install "smart" power strips into which transformers can be plugged. They can sense when the equipment is on or off and turn off power to it accordingly. If you are using older power strips, turn off the power strip to stop the electricity draw when the equipment is not in use.

While many churches are open every day of the week, some of us could use a break when it comes to church meetings. Schedule multiple meetings on one night of the week or month for a more efficient use of the facility. Carpool to reduce driving to and from church.

Follow Up

Share your greening ideas with the pastor, trustees, worship team, and other appropriate leaders.

4. Reuse

"Do not store up for yourselves treasures on earth, where moth and rust consume and where thieves break in and steal; but store up for yourselves treasures in heaven, where neither moth nor rust consumes and where thieves do not break in and steal. For where your treasure is, there your heart will be also."

Matthew 6:19-21

In the last chapter we saw that sabbath lowers our stress, reduces our carbon footprint, and slows us down. This chapter takes it one step further by cutting us loose from much of what drives our busyness: the acquisition of things.

In our culture many of us engage in "retail therapy," but going green asks us to reevaluate our relationship to things. Too much stuff not only depletes us, it depletes the earth and distracts us from serving God. Where our treasure is, there our heart will be also. By turning our focus to reusing what we have instead of constant accumulation of more, we are freer to love the Lord our God and our neighbor as ourselves.

Treasures on Earth

Recently, two of Jerry's beloved *tias* (Spanish for "aunts") passed away within a month of each other. A sister-in-law died from pancreatic cancer during the same time period. Another of Jerry's relatives, a *tio* ("uncle"), is now living in a nursing home. In the midst of this season of sorrow, with its tears and tortillas, memories and meals, we have been dealing with all their possessions. They lived modestly; they did not own anything extravagant. Even so, the amount of stuff they had accumulated is enough to bless many households as it is being redistributed.

Considering their many possessions started me thinking about what Jesus said: "Do not store up for yourselves treasures on earth" (Matthew 6:19a). However, it seems we all do. Most of us have more possessions than we know what to do with. They are stuffed in drawers, closets, garages, extra rooms, and basements. Our stuff is packed on shelves, under beds, and in storage sheds. Finally, our stuff makes its way to the trash. On its way to dumps and landfills, some of it spills over onto roadsides. By the time all is said and done, some of it even finds its way into the oceans. Our stuff is everywhere!

While I do not like to think of myself as a hoarder, lately I have been looking at what I have. I have three large and two small filing cabinets full of notes from the various churches I have served, worship ideas, old bulletins and sermons, tax receipts that go farther back than the Internal Revenue Service can count, old check stubs, calendars dating to college, birthday cards from years ago, and thank-you notes from my earliest days in ministry. It is not like I consult these files often; I just like having them.

Then there are my books. I have so many of them that every other year I need to buy additional bookshelves just to hold them all. I do not read them all; in fact, some of them have never been opened. I purchased some of them simply for the title, such as *Feel the Fear and Do It Anyway*. Others have somehow worked themselves into my identity; parting with them would be too close for comfort. I think fondly of the books I have managed to part with, but I must admit I continue to get the urge to replace them.

In Jesus' day, valuables came in the form of clothing. Precious linens, silks, and other materials were imported from Asia. Yet clothes moths would eat their way through these treasures. Thus Jesus advised against storing up what does not last, "where moth and rust consume and where thieves break in and steal" (Matthew 6:19b).

Today, we have solved much of that problem through "planned obsolescence." We still hoard, but little is constructed to withstand the test of time. What we buy is obsolete in a few years (think electronics and software), or it falls apart before it is eaten by moths or consumed by rust. For the rest of it, we have insurance.

However, not even insurance can protect a person in all situations. In one fast-growing, suburban community in which I served the local church, people live in "McMansions"— extravagant homes with vaulted ceilings, oversized rooms, elaborate rooflines, and three- or four-car garages. These "garage Mahals" are lovely but often too large to furnish. One couple, for example, paid a substantial mortgage while dining on peanut butter and jelly sandwiches in the kitchen, the one room that was furnished. In their case, should thieves break in, there was not anything to steal!

These homes also take a toll on the landscape. Where once people had yards and gardens, giving shelter to birds and sanctuary to wildlife, now the property is covered with hundreds of houses. These houses may give a sense of abundance and wealth, but some of the owners and even the creation have become impoverished.

This impoverishment is common to the possession-oriented life, especially in the matter of time. Between shopping for things, insuring them, guarding them, maintaining them, replacing them, upgrading them, and programming them, we do not have much time left for other people, let alone God. Thus Jesus counsels a different way of living for those who follow him: "Store up for yourselves treasures in heaven" (Matthew

 **Question**

How Much in the World Are You?

Jesus said, "Be in the world but not of the world." When it comes to participating in the consumer culture, how much in the world would you say you are? your congregation?

a. Not at all; we're like the Acts church.
b. Moderate; we practice simple living.
c. Almost all the way in; we keep looking for ways to have more and more.
d. Fully immersed; we have our cake and eat it too!

6:20a). Instead of filling up our bookcases, filing cabinets, and closets, or building homes we cannot afford, Jesus suggests that we invest our money and energy into those things that will last. Note that the word *heaven* as used here is a Jewish way of referring to God. Storing up treasure in heaven, then, means serving others and honoring God by doing so.

There is another meaning lurking here as well. One Bible scholar notes that *store up* and *treasure* come from the same Greek root. The passage literally states, "Treasure up treasures important to God." Translated this way, the treasured object and the treasured location are critical; both of them must be important to God. Nothing fits this meaning better than God's beloved creation—the heavens and the earth and all that is in them. Surely the creation is a treasure to God "where neither moth nor rust consumes and where thieves do not break in and steal" (Matthew 6:20b).

We must be careful about where we invest our energies, "for where your treasure is, there your heart will be also" (Matthew 6:21). This verse is a paradox. It seems logical that our passions would drive our possessions; but, in truth, it is the other way around: Our possessions fuel our passions.

Consider the story of the rich young ruler. After asking how he might inherit eternal life, Jesus lovingly called him to "go, sell what you own, and give the money to the poor, and you will have treasure in heaven; then come, follow me" (Mark 10:21). This bright young man, whose passion seemed to be God's will, grieved over parting with his possessions.

Sometimes we measure our well-being and our status by how much we own; but to paraphrase Jesus, "is not life more than stuff, and the body more than possessions?" (Matthew 6:25b). By looking at us, you would not think so. Yet the Bible envisions a different kind of life for us: a life focused not on what we privately possess but on what we share in common.

All Things in Common

In our individualistic society, what is it that we share in common? I am reminded of the answer every time we sing my favorite hymn, "One Bread, One Body": "And we, though many throughout the earth, / we are one body in this one Lord."[1] Together, we share our membership in the body of Christ. This community of faith guides, challenges, comforts, and shapes us.

65

As important as it is, being part of the body of Christ is not the largest community to which we belong.

Step back a bit, and you will see a bigger picture. As Christians, we are part of an even larger connection: the human family. This human community encompasses every faith tradition; every culture and tribe; every man, woman, and child on earth—friends and enemies alike. Although we may not know or understand one another, our lives are inextricably bound. Yet even this is not our largest common denominator.

Take one more step back, and you will see it. We are part of the living, breathing biosphere. More than anything else, it is the creation we share in common. It is the "ground of our being." As the hymn "I Am Your Mother (Earth Prayer)" suggests, "My health is your health, my wealth is your wealth, / shining with promise, set among stars."[2] The creation itself is the largest community to which we belong.

That is why blogger Matt McDermott points out that going green is not a checklist of deprivations to endure, habits to change, or things to buy. Going green is ultimately about respecting the well-being of every community on earth, from the smallest organisms within our bodies to the grandest natural ecosystems, to the families who live in every corner of the earth. Even future generations who have yet to be born are part of our community.[3]

How we share our common home is a concern of faith. Right now much of the "commons" is marred by our consumer mentality. Our drive for affluence is depleting the earth and depleting us. In an earlier generation, little was thrown away. Dishwater was put on the garden, scraps fed to the farm animals or composted, clothes handed down, and broken items repaired. Shrinkwrap packaging was not yet invented nor even thought necessary. Things were reused until they were all used up. Our grandparents and great-grandparents likely lived by the motto: "Use it up, wear it out, make it do, or do without."

Not so today. "Easy come, easy go" is more like it or "There's more where that came from." To prove it, we have created a whole menu of disposable items, including diapers, cameras, contact lenses, cell phones, lighters, pens, and incomes. For the early church community who shared "all things in common" (Acts 2:44), less was more. For us it seems more is never enough.

While throwaways are incredibly convenient (who misses washing diapers by hand?) and doubtlessly make life easier in the short run, it is the long run that is catching up with us. In a throwaway society, nothing is off limits. We treat the whole earth as disposable, including our fellow human beings.

Magic Mountain

Jerry and I had the opportunity to see the throwaway society close up in 2009 when we went on a Mission Awareness Trip to the Philippines. There we met sixteen-year-old Fadella Mae, whom we had been sponsoring for eight years through the Christian Foundation for Children and Aging (CFCA).[4] Truthfully, we had not been great sponsors over the years. Although we met our monthly financial commitment, we had not written many letters nor sent many pictures. So when we realized Fadella Mae was about to graduate high school and leave the CFCA program, we knew this trip would be our last chance to connect with her.

After securing our tickets, getting our shots, and taking the necessary medication, we took off on a snowy day for the tropical Asian islands halfway around the world. It was not until we were on the long flight over that we realized how much we did not know about the beautiful young woman whose pictures had dotted our refrigerator.

67

One fellow traveler, a Filipino with whom we struck up a conversation, inquired, "Tell me, where does your sponsored daughter live?" Consulting our paperwork, I said, "Payatas." His cheerful expression disappeared. "Oh," he said. "That's where the garbage dump is for Metro Manila. Many people live in the dump. Others make their living off it."

My heart sank. I looked back through the pictures and letters Fadella Mae had sent us over the years. It never occurred to me that this kempt young woman with shiny black hair and a sunny smile might live like that. Her letters had been as positive as her pictures. We were soon to find out what life was like for her.

Meeting Fadella Mae and her family was an exercise in humility. These were strong, faithful, and modest people who live without the financial safety net Jerry and I take for granted. Although poor in things, they are rich in spirit. We were deeply touched by their generosity and gratitude in the midst of unrelenting poverty. It humbled us to realize that our wealth signified a type of hidden poverty. Compared to them, we were rich in things yet poor in spirit.

While Fadella Mae's family did not live in the dump—nicknamed Magic Mountain—they lived in its shadow; and it was a primary source of income. Fadella Mae's brother-in-law, the main wage earner in this family of seven, was a *basurero*, a garbage picker. He would comb the dump's fifty square acres for cans and bottles and whatever else could be resold or salvaged for the family. Her father, although eager to provide, was injured and able to work only intermittently.

Many families in this section of Payatas, called the Promised Land, depended on Magic Mountain for their income. However enchanting its moniker, however, the dump did not live up to its name. It was gray, hazy, blanketed in flies, and dangerous. In 2000, trash was stacked at a seventy-degree angle. Weeks of torrential rains made the 130-foot heap unstable. A horrifying avalanche of trash slid down Magic Mountain onto nearby shanties, killing over 200 people, many of them children. A plaque at the dump's entrance bears witness to their lives.

Bob Hentzen, co-founder and president of CFCA, was the host of our Mission Awareness Trip. Recalling that sickening incident, he pointed to Magic Mountain and said, "That dump is a result of our need for packaging." Items in the Philippines are as heavily packaged as our own and seemingly as disposable. Yet meeting Fadella Mae and her family brought home the point: It is impossible to throw our trash "away." On an increasingly crowded planet, everything goes somewhere, which points to another illusion fostered by the throwaway mentality. We begin to think everything is replaceable; it is not. While you can always buy another disposable pen or razor, scientists do not have a clue about how to fill the aching void in a family whose child has been buried alive in sodden wrappers, plastic bags, cardboard boxes, plastic bottles, cans, and construction debris, such as at Payatas.

The consumer culture is consuming us. Every acre devoted to throwaways is one less acre available for healthy human communities or vibrant life-giving ecosystems. No place and no one is sacred.

In 1968, scientist Garrett Hardin foretold this type of consequence in his ground-breaking article "The Tragedy of the Commons." He predicted that self-interest would trump the common good. Our commons, the natural resources we share in common—such as fresh air, clean water, uncontaminated

 **Spotlight on Science**

A Floating Garbage Patch

The Great Pacific Garbage Patch bobs underneath the surface of the water in the central Pacific Ocean. A perpetual counterclockwise wind current keeps floating debris trapped inside its orbit. It is made up of water bottles, disposable lighters, fishing line, plastic bags, and other plastic items that break into smaller and smaller pieces when exposed to sunlight. Because it shifts and drifts seasonally and much of the trash is shredded slivers of plastic, it is difficult to estimate the size of the dump or to see it from satellites. Yet, after extensive research, some scientists estimate it at twice the size of Texas,[5] while others place it at twice the size of the continental United States.

Although its overall size is in question, its density is not. There are seven times as many fragments of plastic in the dump as there are zooplankton, one of the primary foods for oceanic life. As this plastic confetti permeates the ocean, it attracts poisons such as DDT and PCB to its surfaces. When these fragments of plastic are eaten by birds and fish, they wind up in the bellies of larger fish and continue up the food chain, until women are breastfeeding toxic chemicals to their babies.[6]

Where does all this trash come from? Eighty percent of it migrates to the patch from land, with the remainder coming from cruise ships and other seafaring vessels.[7] As awareness of the patch grows, several organizations are trying to tackle the overwhelming problem of cleanup. While solutions are not yet in sight, you can reduce your impact by eliminating the use of plastic bags and plastic water bottles, avoiding cruise ships that dump waste, and calling for international action. Go to *algalita.com* to follow the progress of research voyages into the Great Pacific Garbage Patch through its interactive Google map and blog.

soils, open spaces, and healthy forests—would suffer. Where we might look to technological breakthroughs to solve the tragedy of the commons, Hardin called for moral breakthroughs.[8]

One moral act is to think carefully about what we buy. Now before I purchase something, I ask myself, Do I need this? How long will it last? Can it be reused? What will I do with it when I am finished? Where will it end up? How will it affect the planet?

As people of faith, it is time to rethink our throwaway mentality. Our current course of continual consumption and planned obsolescence exacts an outrageous price: The poor of the world die that the wealthy may live. We must find a new way.

Abundance, Affluence, and Happiness

The Beatles once sang, "Money can't buy me love." As it turns out, neither can stuff. Some people may equate happiness with the purchase of things. Judging by how much we buy and throw away, it would seem that we are the happiest people on the planet or at least the happiest people in history; but, in reality, we are not.

Author and environmental advocate Bill McKibben says, "A sampling of *Forbes* magazine's 'richest Americans' has happiness scores identical with those of the Pennsylvania Amish. . . . The 'life satisfaction' of pavement dwellers—that is, homeless people—in Calcutta was among the lowest recorded, but it almost doubled when they moved into a slum, at which point they were basically as satisfied with their lives as a sample of college students drawn from forty-seven nations."[9]

Not only is affluence not making us happy, it is making the earth miserable. Planet Earth simply cannot provide for us all. If everyone on earth lived like the average American, it would take about six planets to support us all.[10] While Jesus promised us life abundant, our consumer lifestyle has missed the mark. We have confused "life abundant" with "life affluent."[11]

This is not a new problem. Once, when Jesus was speaking to a crowd, a person called out, "Teacher, tell my brother to divide the family inheritance with me." Jesus resisted getting entangled but had a word for the wise, "Take care! Be on your guard against all kinds of greed; for one's life does not consist in the abundance of possessions" (Luke 12:13, 15).

Consider how the early church handled their possessions: "All who believed were together and had all things in common; they would sell their possessions and goods and distribute the proceeds to all, as any had need" (Acts 2:44-45). This spiritual community reused right from the beginning. Could this sharing of possessions be one of the "many wonders and signs [that were] being done by the apostles"? (Acts 2:43). Certainly, it was a sign of their "glad and generous hearts" (Acts 2:46). Circulating their goods strengthened their commitment to one another and their community.

We rugged individualists, on the other hand, are missing that experience of community. We eat our meals on the run, in the car, standing at the counter, while on the computer, or in front of the television. We may have more money than ever before, but we are also more isolated. Yet studies show that personal connections can stave off death, disease, and divorce. A sense of belonging brings comfort, opportunity, and fellowship; and it is easier on the earth. The more we share, the less the earth has to produce.

However, according to Robert Putnam's *Bowling Alone*, more and more of life is done solo. Since 1975, membership in bowling leagues is down and so is attendance at every other form of social grouping. In chronicling the long breakdown of community, he finds that we are "less likely to join the Rotary, hang out at the bar, or go on picnics"[12] than we used to. We are choosing to be alone while the upside of being with others is that membership in a community has immediate rewards. Simply joining a club or a society of some kind, such as a church, cuts in half the risk of dying in the following year.

The one with the most toys may win, but chances are he or she will die sooner than the one with the most community. Interconnectedness and interdependence are part of life abundant. No matter how much money you may have, affluence can never take the place of abundance.

Interestingly, Putnam's timeline overlaps with the accelerating degradation of the earth. As we retreat from community, the commons suffer; but when we join together, we have a chance to make a profound difference for ourselves and the creation. Thankfully, the fragile economy and our growing awareness of the earth's overtaxed systems are bringing us back to an awareness of our need for community.

Choose to Reuse

With unemployment numbers at a sobering high and the numbers of hungry people climbing, churches are reaching out into the community by hosting meals, food drives, and other programs. Park Hill United Methodist Church in Denver is taking it one step farther. They have always hosted Sunday dinners and other community meals, but they often noticed that too much food was left over. Soon that will be a thing of the past.

Their green team is organizing a garden from which to feed themselves and the community. A compost pile on site will give second life to the excess foods that graced their common table.

Imagine the living communities that will form in the compost pile, in the soil, in the garden, among the gardeners, and among those who share in its bounty.

It all started when a member of the church e-mailed the staff asking hard questions: Why are we still sending out a paper newsletter? When are we going to start recycling? We have big dinners, but we generate lots of throwaways. What are we going

 **Green Fact**

Junk Mail

The average person receives about forty-one pounds of junk mail per year.[13] The average church probably receives more than that. Unsolicited catalogs, magazines, and offers flood church mailboxes every year. Reduce junk mail by going to *directmail.com* and opting out; or call the companies directly who are sending you junk mail, and ask to be removed from their mailing lists.

to do about it? That e-mail gave the church the push it needed. Historically, Park Hill had been on the cutting edge of things. During segregation, the church made the decision to integrate. Blacks and whites have been an active part of the church's leadership and membership ever since. Now sustainability is the important issue; and it is time to become black, white, and green.

In addition to the garden and the compost pile, plans are being made to replace disposable Styrofoam cups with mugs. "Maybe we'll have a mug drive," said Lauren Chance Boyd, adult ministries director. "There are your two favorite mugs and then the forty behind them stacked up in your cabinet. We'll ask people to bring in the ones they're not using so we can reuse them here."

While no one may want your extra mugs as Christmas gifts, regifting is an excellent way to give new life to old things. My friend Jeanette told me that a friend of hers reclaimed a wooden crate from the trash, added foam to the insides, installed hinges on the top, and applied a coat of varnish all around. She then gave it to another friend who now keeps it full of gifts she intends to give away.

Reusing items not only generates creativity, it saves money. What to do with the money you save? "Do not store up for yourself treasures on earth," Jesus said (Matthew 6:19). Instead, invest in something or someone God treasures.

Consider sponsoring a child or an aging person who would otherwise be living off the refuse of society. One dollar per day can transform a person's life. Christian Foundation for Children and Aging (CFCA) not only provides basics such as food, housing assistance, and school fees, but they provide "Clean and Green Projects" that teach biblical stewardship of the earth. Most of all, CFCA creates community for those who would otherwise never meet. Thanks to the gift of sponsorship, Fadella Mae is now entering college, while Jerry and I are learning to walk in solidarity with the poor.

Sharing what we have with others has long been part of the religious consciousness. John the Baptist told a repentant crowd, "Whoever has two coats must share with anyone who has none; and whoever has food must do likewise" (Luke 3:11). Saint Basil the Great, a fourth-century saint revered by the Orthodox Church, picked up on this theme: "The bread which you do not use is the bread of the hungry; the garment hanging in your wardrobe is the garment of him who is naked; the shoes that you do not wear are the shoes of the one who is barefoot; the money that you keep locked away is the money of the poor."[14]

Heeding the wisdom of the saints, innovative ministries have been launched with commonplace, reusable items. Soles4Souls, whose purpose is to change the world one pair of shoes at a time, is one such ministry. The ministry began when Wayne Elsey was home watching coverage of the 2004 Indonesian tsunami on television. He saw one shoe wash up on shore, and it sparked an idea. An executive in the footwear industry, he called his network of friends and asked for shoe donations for the tsunami survivors. The response was overwhelming. After Hurricane Katrina, he called the same group of friends. Over one million pairs of shoes were donated. Elsey realized that people want to help.[15] Now churches are sponsoring "Barefoot Sundays" to raise awareness of people's need for shoes. Gently used shoes can be donated at drop-off points across the country.

In addition to shoes, there is a great need for used blankets. Voice of the Martyrs, a ministry dedicated to helping persecuted Christians worldwide, sends blankets to Sudanese refugees who have been forced from their homes.[16] While the desert is hot during the day, it is cold at night. Often the refugees sleep under the sky with nothing to cover them.

Are your closets full of clothes you never wear? Consider starting a clothing exchange to bless and outfit your community. Kim began one in her church as an inexpensive way of keeping up with the needs of her growing children. Now held twice a year, this festival of second-hand clothing has been expanded to include the whole community. Kim's Mom Ministry gives to those in need while supporting the principle of simple living.

"Most important, though," Kim confided, "it allows me to do what Jesus commanded and clothe those who are 'naked.' Who knows, maybe he or one of his angels have been through those doors a time or two and picked up a couple of things!"

We have so much. Since we cannot take any of it with us when we go, why not bless others now and bless the earth in the process? I am heeding my own advice. In writing this chapter, I have been inspired to pull some of my favorite books off the shelf. I think I know people who would appreciate having them.

What items do you have on your shelves, in your closets, and in your storage sheds that you could give to someone else? Choose to reuse: It is biblical, it is green, and it makes you feel good. After all, there is no need to wait to distribute our things until after we die.

Greening the Church

Reuse

There is no "away." Every time we throw stuff out, it ends up somewhere. We live on a finite planet with finite resources. Our ingenuity and creativity, however, are not finite. Use both as you do the following:

♻ Take a look around your church. What can be reused instead of consumed and thrown away? Can you use mugs instead of Styrofoam, "the good dishes" instead of paper or plastic plates, and real silverware instead of throwaway plastic utensils?

♻ Does the church building occupy land that can also be used in another way? Can space within the church be reused in a way meaningful to the community: used clothing store, meeting space for another church, community garden?

♻ Can you share your summer vacation Bible school curriculum instead of buying new?

♻ Can you share equipment with other churches?

♻ Make a note of all the ways the church reuses things.

Follow Up

Share the information you gathered about reuse with others in your congregation, such as your pastor, trustees, Christian education team, mission committe, and Sunday school classes.

5. Recycle

*To every thing there is a season, and a time to every pur-
pose under the heaven: A time to be born, and a time to die;
a time to plant, and a time to pluck up that which is planted.*
Ecclesiastes 3:1-2 (KJV)

As we saw in the previous chapter, stockpiling things does little good. Our stuff is of no heavenly value; and after a certain
point, it is of no earthly value either. The manufacture, production, and disposal of so much stuff depletes the earth. As
we reclaim our rightful role as stewards of the creation, we see
new ways and opportunities to reduce and reuse. For many persons of faith the answer lies in another *r*: recycling. This practical process of turning one thing into another is biblical to the
core.

The Cycle of Life
Birth, growth, maturation, decline, death: This is the cycle of
life. We can see it at work throughout the universe—from lady-
bugs to trees to stars and in our own lives. As my husband, Jerry,
likes to say, "No one's getting out of here alive." While we might
prefer birth to death, especially when it comes to us and our loved
ones, even death has its place. Actually, though, the cycle of life
does not grind to a halt with death. It merely pauses, dormant,
laying the groundwork for the next cycle to begin.

There is no better place than a garden to observe the cycle
of life up close. My friend Patty has a spacious and colorful

garden. Great blooms of red, white, pink, purple, and yellow flowers surround her house and the edges of her vegetable garden. Peas, beans, lettuce, zucchini, cabbage, tomatoes, potatoes, and carrots flourish in the rich soil there. Sunflowers push up their thick stalks wherever they feel like it, unfurling their tight greenish-yellow heads and lifting them toward the sky.

"The garden is the perfect place to learn about Jesus," Patty told me. "It's even better than a Bible study. Death and resurrection are all over the place." With that invitation, I began my apprenticeship. I have always wanted to be a farmer, but I have had no real experience. Even as a botany student in college, I did not have much of a green thumb. My houseplants teetered between zealously over-watered and forgetfully neglected. Patty, an experienced gardener, is introducing me to the real-life wonders of growing things.

As we hoe, plant, weed, water, and weed some more, I have noticed that the garden is in constant flux. Patty is right: Life and death are always giving way to each other. Not long ago, Patty noticed a two-foot-tall spinach plant growing out of the decaying matter in the compost pile. She surveyed it, plucked it out of the ground, and gave it to me—stalk and all. I brought it home, and that night Jerry and I ate delicious steamed spinach for dinner.

Nothing is wasted in the garden, not even death. Hay is used as mulch to keep moisture in the soil and suppress the growth of weeds. Eventually it breaks down and is absorbed by the soil, enriching it. Once the vegetables growing up through the hay are harvested, any remains go in the compost pile to decompose. After awhile, the remains biodegrade, forming a rich soil-like mixture. Next spring that organic matter will be worked into the garden soil to release nutrients such as carbon, nitrogen, and phosphorous. In turn, those nutrients will be absorbed by next year's zucchini and tomatoes, the stalks of which will wind up in next year's compost pile—and the cycle of life will continue.

This cycling of life is the foundation upon which all of creation functions, so I suppose it is no coincidence that in the Bible, God is portrayed as a gardener. In the garden of Eden, it was the Lord who formed living beings out of the soil (Genesis 2:7), reminding Adam that "you are dust / and to dust you shall return" (Genesis 3:19). God finally declares the end of the cycle by turning humans back into humus, saying, "Turn back, you mortals" (Psalm 90:3), as our bodies are returned to the ground. It seems to me that recycling, adopted by households in the 1960's as a response to the throwaway society,[1] is actually a biblical concept. The word *recycle* can be thought of as "to come full circle." According to the Scriptures, that is exactly what our bodies do. Could it be that the Gardener of Eden instituted recycling?

Nowhere do we see the cycle of life more powerfully than in the life and death of Jesus. If recycling is transfiguring something old into something new, then resurrection is the ultimate in recycling! One bumper sticker sighted in New York City says, "Resurrection—God's Recycling Plan."

New Life for Trash

Just as "death has been swallowed up in victory" through resurrecton (1 Corinthians 15:54), the waste we generate can be swallowed up in victory through recycling. No more dead ends for our trash. Can you see it? Recycling is holy and wholly biblical. William McDonough and Michael Braungart, authors of *Cradle to Cradle: Remaking the Way We Make Things*, write, "Waste is a man-made creation since there is no garbage in nature."[2] Nature recycles waste automatically. In Patty's garden, all is

81

resurrected. We humans, on the other hand, have to be intentional about it. When we recycle, we fall into step with the cycle of life set in motion by God at the beginning.

However, there is a huge waste stream that slips through the cracks between those who do and those who do not recycle. Americans throw out almost two million plastic bottles per hour, and only about one in four bottles are recycled.[3] Moreover, those bottles that wind up in the trash can or litter the side

Question

What About Recycling?

Rate your recycling habits.

    a. I am a recycling fool. Nothing winds up in the trash.

    b. I recycle everything I can, and I buy recycled products.

    c. I recycle when it is convenient, but I do not go out of my way to do so.

    d. There is so much trash in the world, what difference does it make?

    e. I am a litterbug and proud of it.

of the road are not just a waste issue; they are a national security issue. We fight wars over petroleum. How many soldiers and civilians have to die for us to have the right to toss those single-use bottles? Recycling reduces our dependence on foreign oil. That makes recycling a positive approach to national security and human welfare.

In addition to the national-security, humanitarian, and ecological reasons to recycle, there is also money to be made in recycling. For example, beverage cans made from aluminum can be made and remade from the same aluminum indefinitely; continued recycling does not diminish the aluminum's quality. Yet each year an estimated 36 billion aluminum cans wind up in landfills.[4] At 15 cents per pound, that translates to $540 million worth of buried treasure. Collecting aluminum cans would be easy money for church missions, outreach, and other programs. Recycling the cans requires no special skills, and any age group can participate. Plus removing the cans that litter our highways and other public lands would beautify the earth.

The benefits of recycling, of course, do not end with money. Add to the list energy savings, more open spaces, fewer dumps, and the conservation of natural resources for future generations, not to mention a reduction in air and water pollution. The impact is local and global, social and financial, theological and ethical.

Consider how many plastic bottles, aluminum cans, steel cans, newspapers, and milk jugs, and how much office and copy paper, cardboard, and glass your household goes through in a day, a week, a month, a year. Now multiply that by the number of people in your congregation. Take that figure and multiply it by all the churches and houses of worship in your community. If we, as people of faith, took seriously that recycling is at the heart of creation and at the heart of the Christian life, we could make a tremendous difference in the world. Sisters and brothers in Christ, it is time to turn trash into cash.

In Yakima, Washington, one church is doing just that. Over the past 30 years, Wesley United Methodist Church has saved five million pounds of material from going into the landfill. They process about 60,000 pounds of recyclables per month. Last year their efforts brought in $20,000. Before you decide that is too much work, think about this: The average age of their core recycling group is 76 years old![5]

Downcycling, Upcycling, and Resurrection

Hauling off our recyclables to the curbside or nearest recycling center is not the end of the story on recycling. If sustainability, or the capacity of all creation to endure, is the goal for going green, this alone will not get us there because much of recycling is actually downcycling, especially when it comes to plastics. Recycling #1 plastic bottles, the kind you drink water or soda out of, will not get you new #1 plastic bottles. Those bottles will be turned into lower-grade plastics until they cannot be recycled again, and then they will be trashed.

Downcycling still saves energy, water, and habitat while reducing pollution and stress on the environment. It also leads to cleaner neighborhoods. So do not stop downcycling simply because the materials cannot be recycled indefinitely. The point is that downcycling alone will not get us to sustainability because industries will still have to mine the earth, extract resources, cut down timber, and disrupt human and creature communities in order to keep making new products.

While downcycling slows that process down, upcycling turns it around. Upcycling actually improves the quality or value of an item the second time around. Shipping containers that may transport everything from clothing to foodstuffs to electronics are now being converted into office space, living space, malls, and luxury condos.[6] Paper products are being made into jewelry, kitchenware, pens, and pencils. Plastic bottles are made into fleece jackets. Upcycling reduces waste and improves the quality of life.

TerraCycle, a company that specializes in upcycling, has a special connection to churches. Using formerly non-recyclable material such as computer disks, vinyl billboards, juice pouches, and candy wrappers, these innovative entrepreneurs manufacture items such as lunchboxes, backpacks, notepads, notebooks, and pencil pouches. Not only are they reducing the American

---

Spotlight on Science

Close the Loop

Recycling is good; buying recycled products is even better. It "closes the loop" and creates a larger market for these items, eventually bringing the price down. You may pay more up front; but consider that purchasing paper made from virgin fiber has its costs, too, albeit hidden.

♻ When shopping for computer paper, look for "post-consumer waste" (PCW) on the package, which indicates that recycled materials are being used in its manufacture. "Pre-consumer waste" means that scrap materials left over from the original manufacturing process were used. Purchasing items with the highest PCW content available saves the most trees, energy, greenhouse gas emissions, and water possible and reduces air and water pollution.

♻ Recycling one short ton of paper saves 17 mature trees, 7,000 gallons of water, three cubic yards of landfill space, two barrels of oil, and 4,000 kilowatt-hours of electricity.[9]

♻ Recycling causes 35 percent less water pollution and 74 percent less air pollution than making virgin paper.

♻ Paper products are the largest component of municipal solid waste, making up more than 40 percent of the composition of landfills. Most of it is used in packaging.[10]

---

waste stream, they are generating a revenue stream. They pay church groups and other volunteer organizations to collect the specific items needed. Their goal is to turn trash into a valuable commodity through "eco-economics."[7]

Creative Christian mothers in Payatas, Philippines, the home of the Magic Mountain dump, have already discovered a way to do this. While on our Mission Awareness Trip there, we received beautiful handmade crafts and gifts. One gift in particular stood out: sturdy tote bags made from used juice pouches. Normally used once and then discarded, these bright orange and purple packages were picked off the trash heap, washed, and sewn together in such a way that they are now brightly colored, attractive bags. The women sell the tote bags to feed their families. What a grand example of upcycling for the mothers, for their families, and for the earth.

What is great about upcycling is that it resembles resurrection for the material world. Just as our bodies go into the ground perishable and come out imperishable, or go in weak and come out powerful, or go in physical and come out spiritual, so these single-use packages are upgraded into objects of greater beauty and lasting value. It seems that God not only invented recycling, in Jesus Christ, God became the first upcycler. If you have had any doubts, lay them aside: God is green!

In fact, the Christian life is a perfect example of upcycling. Through Christ our sinful ways are sanctified, our weaknesses become our strengths, and our downfall becomes our witness. Peter denied Christ three times and then became the rock upon which the church was built. Paul killed Christians and then became the apostle to the apostles. That is spiritual upcycling.

It is not for nothing we are saved but to add value and beauty to the world. "Listen, I will tell you a mystery!" Paul writes. "We will not all die, but we will all be changed (1 Corinthians 15:51). We are being repurposed by God for something greater: "He died for all, so that those who live might live no longer for themselves, but for him who died and was raised for them" (2 Corinthians 5:15).

Green Church

In Christ, our lives are sanctified and redeemed. What if our buildings reflected that? What if sanctuaries, cathedrals, and houses of worship were built or rebuilt to reflect the upcycled, resurrected life? Can you imagine a church building that resurrects the creation and the natural systems instead of degrading them or pushing them aside?

St. Mark's Presbyterian Church in Newport Beach, California, not only imagined an upcycled, resurrected church, but they built it. Dubbed "The Greenest New Church in America" by Audubon International, this church aims to practice what it preaches. Thanks to the church's Ecophilia (meaning "a friendly feeling for the environment") Committee, the building and its campus are green. With over 500 trees on the grounds and many drought-resistant native plants, the congregation created habitat for a diversity of birds and wildlife. An onsite nature center is open to the public to teach the community about caring for creation. Even the parking lot is green; a specially constructed system recaptures oil to prevent it from entering the local water supply.

The building meets the high-energy efficiency standards of Audubon International and LEED (Leadership in Energy and Environmental Design) certification. Designed to allow in as much natural lighting as possible, the building also makes use of energy-efficient windows that open. Tankless water heaters provide instant heat. Graceful curved pews are made from tree-farmed wood rather than virgin timber.[8]

Holy Redeemer Catholic School in Portland, Oregon, has taken greening a step further. The roof of the John Paul II Hall is now alive with growing plants. These "living" roofs provide habitat for birds and butterflies, reduce heating and cooling costs, improve air quality, reduce local heat islands in urban settings, and cut down on storm-water runoff.[11] This type of green space also provides beauty and a place to grow food.

Green Fact

Recycling

Nothing lasts forever, but some things last longer than others.[13]

Aluminum cans	500 years
Glass bottles	4,000+ years
Nylon fabric	30-40 years[14]
Leather	Up to 50 years
Orange and banana peels	Up to 2 years
Tin cans	50 years
Plastic bags	10-20 years
Plastic six-pack holders	100 years
Plastic bottles	Indefinitely

On average, it costs $30 per ton to recycle trash, $50 to send it to the landfill, or $65 to $75 to incinerate it.[15]

If you think your vestry, session, or trustees are too "old school" to approve of greening your church, think again. The historic Arbroath Abbey in Scotland, which dates back to the twelvth century, has now incorporated a living roof as well.[12]

One Thing Leads to Another

You do not have to be the greenest Christian in the world or worship at the greenest church to make a difference, to show that you care for creation, or to prove your love of God. Just start where you are, and trust God for the results.

Years ago, I started a recycling program in the town where I used to live in Vermont. I also tried to start one at a synagogue I attended. Although I was an active recycler at first, over the years—except for the occasional phone book—I simply fell out of the habit. Ten years ago, I was not recycling anything at all. It was not until my friend Neeva came to visit and offered to haul my newspapers off to the recycling center that I once again started to recycle consistantly. Every time she came to visit, she would take the newspapers there. After a while, just looking at the newspapers reminded me of the recycling center; and I took them there myself. Over time, I began to recycle not only newspapers but cans, glass, and plastic. Then I figured out how to recycle cardboard, paper, printer cartridges, and electronics.

Finally, this new commitment began to work its way into my preaching. One Sunday morning I talked about recycling as a way to care for God's creation. If I remember correctly, there were not that many people in attendance; and nobody shouted hallelujah at the end of my sermon. I thought the sermon was a dud. However, the sermon did touch at least one person in the congregation. Dave, the president of the men's ministry, had played a part in the first Earth Day in his community some thirty years earlier. The sermon reminded him of his own convictions that had fallen by the wayside.

Dave decided that the church's United Methodist Men group ought to pick up recyclables from older members in the church and transport them to the recycling center. So on the third Saturday of every month, he and several men would collect cardboard boxes, piles of newspapers, plastic bottles, glass jars, and the occasional beer can to take to the local recycling center. It did not seem like much, but it filled a need in the community.

It filled a need for Dave, too. Always full of ideas, Dave started his own recycling business. Driving an old truck especially outfitted for recycling (he calls it the Clampett-mobile in honor of Jed Clampett and *The Beverly Hillbillies*), Dave says, "I'm just a taxicab for trash." Dave may not realize it, but actually he is a steward of the creation; and he is helping an entire community to be stewards as well. The results of the community's stewardship have been positive: Business has tripled over the last several years for him and for the recycling center.

It did not end there, however. Dave is president of the school board. Combining his creation-care ethic and his love of children, he designed a "Kick Butt" Earth Day for the sixth graders. The idea was to help children say no to tobacco while taking care of the earth. The day involved picking up trash in the open places surrounding the middle school. The program was so successful that after the students learned how Styrofoam does not biodegrade, how it releases carcinogens when heated, and how their disposable lunch trays were made of it, they asked why the school district was still using items made of Styrofoam.

The students spoke up forcefully and requested non-toxic trays in the lunchroom; and they made a presentation at an evening school board meeting, including a play they had written. The board voted unanimously to find the money to provide trays made from different material, and the board has kept their promise.

Meanwhile, Dave developed a worm-based composting operation in Rawlins, Wyoming, that will compost the new trays. Soon, the children will be able to take field trips to watch the process in action. Now Dave is talking with the city about curbside recycling. And to think that it all started with Neeva hauling my newspaper to the recycling center! One thing certainly leads to another. Given a chance, most people want to do right by the earth. Sometimes they just need a nudge. Who knows, that nudge may come from someone like you.

Life is short. While our aluminum cans may be around forever, we will not, at least not with these bodies. So make the most of what you have, and do the most with what you have. Patty has a garden and a compost pile. St. Mark's Presbyterian Church has an Ecophilia Committee. TerraCycle has a creative streak. The mothers in Payatas have resourcefulness. Neeva has a desire to be helpful. Dave has a Clampett-mobile. What do you have?

Whatever you have, do not let it go to waste. No matter your gift or passion, God has blessed you with it for the good of all creation. As you use your gifts, remember that you will not be going it alone. You have God's parent-like support. "As a father has compassion for his children, / so the LORD has compassion for those who fear him. / For he knows how we were made; / he remembers that we are dust" (Psalm 103:13-14).

One day, we will be imperishable, glorious, powerful, and spiritual. Together with Jesus we will inhabit a new heaven and new earth. In the meantime, though, we are somewhere between dust and dust; but do not let that get you down—even dust can make a difference. Just as a garden cycles life, let God's gifts flow through you for the good of all—for us and future generations.

Recycling at Church

Does your church participate in the cycle of life by recycling?

- Make a list of all the materials your church receives or generates that could be recycled: bulletins, catalogues, newsletters, kitchen waste, paper, and other materials.

- Note which of the items from the list above that your church is already recycling.

- What will it take to begin a recycling program at your church? What kind of bins will you need and where? Will you need signs? How will the recyclables get to the recycling center?

- Close the loop by purchasing recycled products. Doing so creates a steady market for recycled goods. Check to see if bulletins, paper towels, toilet paper, and napkins are made of recycled paper. Are plastic bags made of recycled content? Look closely at the label. What percentage of the recycled content is post-consumer waste and what percentage is pre-consumer waste?

- A garden is a great place to observe the cycle of life. Start a garden on church grounds, and invite your community to participate.

- Compost/recycle food scraps for use in the garden.

Follow Up

Share your findings with the pastor, trustees, mission committee, and other interested church leaders.

6. Rejoice!

Then I saw a new heaven and a new earth; for the first heaven and the first earth had passed away, and the sea was no more. And I saw the holy city, the new Jerusalem, coming down out of heaven from God, prepared as a bride adorned for her husband.

Revelation 21:1-2

We began GREEN CHURCH by talking about the need to repent from our creation-destroying ways and to reclaim our role as stewards of creation. We have looked at how reusing, reducing, and recycling are biblical responses to the environmental crises we face. Now it is time to rejoice! You might think that is an odd response to the challenging themes of this study, but rejoicing affirms our faith in the promises of God and our role as co-creators with God.

God Is a Nature Lover

In 2007, the Wyoming Association of Churches went out on a limb. Together with the Wyoming Conservation Voters Education Fund, this organization co-hosted a statewide gathering called "On Sacred Ground: Faith and the Environment." The gathering was held at a log community center in Lander, Wyoming, encompassed by a semi-circle of stunning mountain ranges.

While it seemed like an unlikely partnership—neither Christians nor environmentalists are in the majority in this sparsely populated state, and each group tends to be suspicious of the other—it was a success. That splendid autumn weekend found almost two hundred people in attendance. It was a glorious mix of church women and conservationists, lay leaders and ranchers, Sunday school teachers and wildlife advocates. There were also high school teachers and students present along with quite a few pastors there, with an eco-justice theologian and an evangelical preacher-turned-environmental-activist thrown in for good measure. Not all of us shared a common language, but we did share a common bond: love of the place we call home and a concern for its health.

Wyomingites love the land, the wildlife, the wide-open spaces, the sky, the solitude, and even the wind. You have to, otherwise there is not much reason to live here. With just five people per square mile and little competition from trees, buildings, or billboards, that is about all there is—except for the ubiquitous natural gas wells, oil wells, oil refineries, coal mines, trona mines, coal-fired power plants, and wind turbines.

Yet as much as each one of us, and indeed people everywhere, love the earth, God loves it even more. In *Good Goats: Healing Our Image of God*, the authors make the point that "God loves us at least as much as the person who loves us the most."[1] If that is true about humankind, it must be true of the rest of creation as well. After all, didn't God pronounce the whole of creation very good? That means God loves the whole creation at least as much as any one of us possibly could whether rancher, backyard gardener, or evangelical preacher-turned-environmental-activist. While our love is conditional (who loves mosquitoes?), God loves it all fiercely: mosquitoes, mountains, ocean depths, bird songs, rocky riverbanks, humans, puppies, owls, sunflowers, rain, starry nights, sandy beaches, wind-driven snow, and fossil fuels.

The Scriptures affirm the extent of God's love: "For God so loved the world that he gave his only Son" (John 3:16). Consider the fact that *world* is a translation of the Greek *kosmon*, from which we get *cosmos* or *universe*.[2] World includes not just humankind, but everything from the farthest star to the smallest flower. I would say God is a nature lover.

God's love for the world is not a one-way affair; the feelings are mutual. "The heavens declare the glory of God; / the skies proclaim the work of his hands" (Psalm 19:1, NIV). In fact, all the works of the Lord give thanks to God, even the most unlikely ones. "Praise the LORD from the earth, / you sea monsters and all deeps, / fire and hail, snow and frost, / stormy wind fulfilling his command! / Mountains and all hills, fruits trees and all cedars! / Wild animals and all cattle, / creeping things and flying birds!" (Psalm 148:7-10). I am not exactly sure how a sea monster or hail praises God; but I imagine it comes naturally, the way a child loves her mother.

The relationship between Creator and creation did not end on Day 6 back in Genesis. God did not create the heavens and earth and then step back and say, "Hey, good luck, now you're on your own!" The relationship is ongoing. God sustains the creation, and the creation praises God by thriving and flourishing. At least that is the ideal scenario.

However, much of the creation is not thriving or flourishing. Today, much of it is being pushed out of existence, manipulated for human gain, and degraded to the point of nonfunctionality. The earth does not always "make a joyful noise to the LORD" (Psalm 100:1); sometimes it is more like an anguished cry. What else would you call the thundering ice-quakes on Greenland as 10,000-year-old ice plates melt, shift, and rumble into the surrounding sea? or the whimper of exhausted polar bears that can no longer find floating ice on which to rest in the Arctic Circle? or the gasp of suddenly home-less families whose coastal abodes are washed out to sea by ris-ing tides? or the cries of parents whose children are buried alive by trash landslides in urban garbage dumps?

"We know that the whole creation has been groaning" (Romans 8:22), Paul wrote to the church at Rome; and that was long before the sins against creation that we manufacture today. Even now "the creation waits with eager longing for the reveal-ing of the children of God" (Romans 8:19).

God Makes All Things New

God is not oblivious to these cries. Because of God's care for the creation, God intends for it to "be set free from its bondage to decay" (Romans 8:21). In the Hebrew Bible and the New Testament, we hear the prophetic promise of a creation restored. "I am about to do a new thing," Isaiah prophesies, "now it springs forth, do you not perceive it? / I will make a way in the wilderness / and rivers in the desert" (Isaiah 43:19). "See, I am making all things new" (Revelation 21:5), the Holy One affirms. What is this new thing? I believe I caught a glimpse of it recently.

My friend Jenita and I hiked the Uplift, that small ridge of mountains that runs through my town. It was a hot, dry morn-ing—unusual this summer. We have had more rain this year than we have had in a long time. The moisture has transformed the high-desert plains; brown has given way to green. A few rivers have even flooded. After reaching the crest of the ridge, we turned and looked back over the valley. A velvety green carpet stretched out before us, running across the valley floor and up the mountains on the far side some thirty miles away.

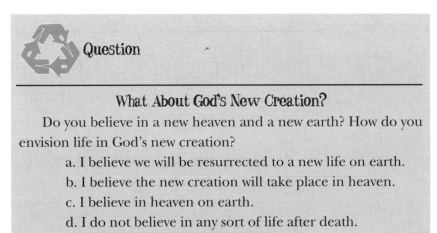

Question

What About God's New Creation?

Do you believe in a new heaven and a new earth? How do you envision life in God's new creation?

    a. I believe we will be resurrected to a new life on earth.
    b. I believe the new creation will take place in heaven.
    c. I believe in heaven on earth.
    d. I do not believe in any sort of life after death.
    e. I am not sure what I believe.

Seattle, it is not. Nevertheless my heart rejoiced. It has been many years since we have seen such greenery here. Years of drought had dried out the soil and hardened the landscape. Without moisture even our souls had grown parched. Now wildflowers, long dormant, have pushed up through the sandy soil. Bursts of color are scattered among the sagebrush.

As I surveyed the glorious works of God, another prophecy of Isaiah floated up to my consciousness: "The wilderness and the dry land shall be glad, / the desert shall rejoice and blossom; / like the crocus it shall blossom abundantly, / and rejoice with joy and singing" (Isaiah 35:1-2). It was as if the Scriptures had come to life before my eyes. Yet, the color-flecked carpet of new life is just a hint of what is to come. There is much more.

Consider Isaiah's vision of the Peaceable Kingdom in which life will be transfigured: "The wolf shall live with the lamb, /

the leopard shall lie down with the kid, / the calf and the lion and the fatling together, / and a little child shall lead them" (Isaiah 11:6). Predator and prey will peacefully coexist, and the most vulnerable among us will be safe.

The Peaceable Kingdom is not the only vision of creation restored. Images abound in the Bible. Most hopeful is this one: "For I am about to create new heavens / and a new earth; / the former things shall not be remembered / or come to mind. / But be glad and rejoice forever / in what I am creating" (Isaiah 65:17-18).

This promise of new heavens and a new earth is no incidental statement or one-time pledge. It is twice declared in the Hebrew Bible and twice in the New Testament, most famously here in Revelation 21:1: "Then I saw a new heaven and a new earth; for the first heaven and the first earth had passed away."

For those of us who grieve deeply the changing climates, who mourn the silencing of birds and the disappearance of fish, who are horrified by our throwaway attitude toward fellow human beings, and who reject the fouling of our nest, this promise is cause for rejoicing! Rather than doom and gloom, a bright picture of hope shines on us from the future. To know that all of history is moving toward renewal of the entire creation with God at the helm, fills us, too, with "eager longing."

You may be thinking, *If God will one day create a new heaven and new earth, doesn't that let us off the hook when it comes to environmental stewardship? If God has it all covered, why should we bother going green? Let God take care of it.* James Watt, former US Secretary of the Interior, expressed a similar sentiment: "We don't have to protect the environment, the Second Coming is at hand."[3] Paul anticipated a similar "why bother" response from his audience when he spoke to them about eternal life in

Christ: "Should we continue in sin in order that grace may abound? By no means! How can we who died to sin go on living in it?" (Romans 6:1-2).

Likewise, now that we have repented from our destructive behaviors toward the creation and reclaimed our role as stewards, how can we go back to our old ways? As caretakers of the creation, we are co-creators with God, fellow workers with the Lord. The creation is waiting in eager expectation, not for divine redemption but for "the appearing of the children of God." Somehow, God is working out renewal for the created order through us. For that reason, we are to be "steadfast, immovable, always excelling in the work of the Lord, because you know that in the Lord your labor is not in vain" (1 Corinthians 15:58).

Bishop N. T. Wright, a noted bible scholar, teases out Paul's underlying meaning: "What you *do* in the present—by painting, preaching, singing, sewing, praying, teaching, building hospitals, digging wells, campaigning for justice, writing poems, caring for the needy, loving your neighbor as yourself—*will last into God's future.*"[4] This future, God's future, is what he calls, "life after life after death."[5] We will then enjoy resurrected life with Jesus in the new heavens and the new earth, the restored creation.

Earth Rise

In some ways, our vision of this restoration began on Christmas Eve 1968. That is when our collective vision of heaven and earth began to change. The *Apollo 8* spacecraft circled the moon to scout out landing sites for the upcoming *Apollo 11* mission that would eventually put the first man on the moon. As part of its explorations, *Apollo 8* flew around the dark side of the moon, lost radio contact—as was expected—and reemerged, to the great relief of NASA command on the ground.

As the spaceship reestablished radio contact, the astronauts looked up from their computer monitors and saw Earth, a brilliant blue and white globe rising out of the dark, formless void of space. It was an awesome moment. Mission commander Frank Borman even read from the Book of Genesis: "In the beginning God created the heaven and the earth."

That image did not remain in space. Someone snapped a picture of our planet. Once published, the photograph, entitled *Earth Rise*, changed human consciousness forever. Although we had been on our way to explore the moon, for the first time ever we saw Earth.

Anne Morrow Lindbergh noted, "Man had to free himself from earth to perceive both its diminutive place in a solar system and its inestimable value as a life-fostering planet. As [inhabitants of earth], we may have taken another step into adulthood. We can see our planet earth with detachment, with tenderness, with some shame and pity, but at last also with love."[6]

The same kind of love with which God loves the cosmos began to well up in us. Taylor Wang, a scientist who flew the 1983 Spacelab Mission said, "A Chinese tale tells of some men sent to harm a young girl who, upon seeing her beauty, become her protectors rather than her violators. That's how I felt seeing the Earth for the first time. I could not help but love and cherish her."[7]

Our love has manifested itself in the care of creation, or at least in a growing awareness of it. According to Al Gore in his book *An Inconvenient Truth*, "Within two years of this picture being taken, the modern environmental movement was born. The Clean Air Act, the Clean Water Act, the Natural Environmental Policy Act, and the first Earth Day all came about within a few years of this picture being seen for the first

Spotlight on Science

Your Carbon Footprint

What is a carbon footprint? I like this definition: "Your carbon footprint is the sum of all CO_2 emissions that are directly and indirectly associated with your activities over a given time frame (usually a year)."[8] In fact, a carbon footprint can be calculated for a person, a family, a congregation, a nation, an event, or a particular product.

Not every person or every nation has the same carbon footprint. Compare the following annual household averages:[9]

54,600 pounds of CO_2 — United States
27,700 pounds of CO_2 —Germany
4,600 pounds of CO_2 —Sweden
10,600 pounds of CO_2 —Mexico
400 pounds of CO_2 —Kenya.

The United States, with only four percent of the world's population, produces about 20 percent of the world's carbon emissions from the burning of fossil fuels. (China, with about 1/6 of the world's population, produces about 22 percent.) In the United States, most people enjoy a high standard of living; and our carbon footprint is proof of that. Reducing our carbon footprint would have a tremendously positive impact on the world as a whole.

While the idea of a carbon footprint may still seem mysterious, calculating it is not. Online calculators from extremely technical to super easy can help determine a person's carbon footprint. Check out the following calculators for more information:

Low Carbon Diet: *empowermentinstitute.net/lcd/* (easy)

Native Energy: *nativeenergy.com* (easy and medium options)

Cool Congregation: *coolcongregations.com* (technical)

Once you have calculated the carbon footprint of your church, you can then reduce it by reducing your carbon-producing activities. For more on that, see the companion volume: *7 Simple Steps to Green Your Church.*

time."[8] Edgar Mitchell, the sixth person to walk on the moon, said, "We went to the Moon as technicians; we returned as humanitarians."[9]

In the intervening years, *Earth Rise* has also begun to change our theology. Seeing that we all inhabit one small planet suspended in the cold silence of space, church missions have taken on a new note of cross-cultural respect. Interreligious dialogue has begun in earnest. We are even reading the Scriptures with new eyes. Now that we have flown in the heavens, walked on the moon, and set our sights on Mars, our consciousness has expanded. As our cosmology changes, so does our theology.

We look again at the promises of a new heaven and a new earth, and we see something we never saw before: It is not a vision of life after death that takes place up there somewhere; it is a vision of life after life after death. This is the resurrection the ancients envisioned happening right here on earth. In other words, salvation is not so much going to heaven when we die but about heaven coming to earth. Salvation includes a profound harmony with God, the creation, and one another.

Good News to the Whole Creation

"Go into all the world and proclaim the good news to the whole creation" (Mark 16:15). This is the commission of the resurrected Jesus in the Gospel of Mark. Many disciples are already heeding the call.

Wangari Maathai, a Kenyan professor and activist, has been involved with community-based tree planting since 1977. She noticed that the forests in her native land were being cut down for private gain, but their loss impoverished the larger community and made life especially hard for the women. Depleted forests made it more difficult to collect firewood, harvest fruit, and make medicines. Also the soil eroded, water tables dropped, and the weather changed. Meanwhile, the people's health and morale plummeted.

On World Environment Day 1977, Maathai planted seven trees. What started out as a symbolic act on behalf of the women became a far-reaching movement called the Greenbelt Project.

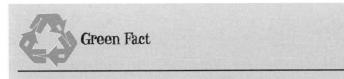

Green Fact

Plant a Tree

A single tree will absorb one ton of carbon dioxide over its lifetime. Shade provided by trees can also reduce your air conditioning bill by ten to fifteen percent. Planting trees is one way to go carbon-neutral.

It now includes over 6,000 women's groups who have planted over 30 million trees throughout Kenya and beyond. This grassroots movement has made such a difference for so many people that Maathai was awarded the 2004 Nobel Peace Prize. She was the first African woman and the first environmentalist to receive this honor.

When Maathai heard the news of the honor, she planted a tree. "That's the way I do things," she said. "When I want to celebrate I plant a tree!" She would like others to do the same. Her goal is one billion new trees per year. "For the last few years," she explained, "I have been trying to communicate with leaders of various Christian churches to urge them to bring protection and conservation of the environment into the mainstream of their faith and their teachings. I have been suggesting that Easter Monday could be a very good day for the entire Christendom to plant trees. If we could make that Monday a day of regeneration, revival, of being reborn, of finding salvation by restoring the Earth, it would be a great celebration of Christ's resurrection. After all, Christ was crucified on the cross. In a light touch, I always say, somebody had to go into the forest, cut a tree, and chop it up for Jesus to be crucified. What a great celebration of his conquering [death] it would be if we were to plant trees on Easter Monday in thanksgiving."[12]

While Maathai leads an international effort to plant trees in honor of the Resurrection, members of Nashville's Christ Church Cathedral Environmental Ministry are cleaning up the Cumberland River as a sign of hope. "In Christianity, water symbolizes the hope of renewal," says Joyce Wilding, the church's environmental minister. "Water itself conveys this spiritual meaning through its properties of cleansing and healing. Yet we continue to destroy watersheds and contaminate many semi-pristine water sources. What does it mean when water is so scarce that our primary symbol of renewal is no longer available? Or when water is so contaminated that its capacity to heal has been lost?"[13]

What does it mean when water is so expensive that it is not affordable for the poor? That is the case with bottled water. Not only does it deplete underground aquifers, drain wetlands, and generate billions of empty plastic bottles that are never disposed of, bottled water can be up to 1,000 to 10,000 times more expensive than tap water, while often being no cleaner or safer. Gallon for gallon, bottled water is even more expensive than gasoline.[14] As aquifers are drained, bottled water makes natural water less available for the poor of the world. With this in mind, members of the Environmental Ministry at Christ Church Cathedral are encouraging others to stop buying bottled water. Instead, members use and refill stainless steel canisters. The Cathedral now no longer purchases bottled water for its events.

From trees to water, there are many ways to renew creation. Not much is needed to get started. Sometimes all it takes is one little fish.

When the endangered Watercress Darter, a tiny multicolored fish, was discovered in the marshy springs on its church property, Faith Apostolic Church in Birmingham, Alabama, decided to join forces with local groups to protect it. Biology professors and church members are excited about what is to come. Having signed a memorandum of understanding with several other organizations interested in preserving the fish, the congregation will now be home to a park, a meditation garden, and an center that will educate the community and allow it to draw closer to the beauty of creation. Church members are helping to clean up the area by removing invasive species and restoring native plants as well as being trained in water-quality testing.[15]

What About You?

Churches are moving beyond their four walls to embrace and bless the natural world around them along with the people who live there. Even now, persons of faith are envisioning a new heaven and new earth and daring to live into that shining future.

What about you? Have you ventured beyond the four walls of your church? Who or what do you see when you do? Do you see concrete or pavement, meadows or mountains, subdivisions or sky? Do you see the homeless or McMansions?

Take a good look. Who knows what is in the marshy swamps, rivers, streams, forests, and weed patches around your church. Who knows what is in the hearts and minds of the poor in your community. Do not ignore it; explore it. You just may find the key to your church's connection to creation.

If you would like to help start a green movement in your church, you might consider getting a small handbook that complements the information in this book, called *7 Simple Steps to Green Your Church*. It shows, step by step, what your church can do to care for the creation.

While you are exploring, remember to rejoice! Although the work before us is demanding, it will call us to our best selves. Even when it seems that the road is long and progress is hard to come by, remember that "in the Lord, your labor is not in vain." Somehow, God is using us to free the creation from the bondage of decay. Let the joy of that promise pull you, and the creation, forward into God's good future.

As you go out to "proclaim the good news to the whole creation" (Mark 16:15), take with you this blessed image of the renewed creation: For you shall go out in joy, / and be led back in peace; / the mountains and the hills before you / shall burst into song, / and all the trees of the field shall clap their hands" (Isaiah 55:12).

Share Your Joy

- ♻ If your congregation has made changes in energy consumption during this time, recalculate your carbon footprint. Post the results.

- ♻ Design and make paraments or worship banners that reflect your renewed commitment to care for creation.

- ♻ Write a hymn, poem, play, or liturgical dance that highlights your commitment to care for creation.

- ♻ Arrange to give your testimony in church about your new understandings and commitments toward the care of creation.

- ♻ Plant a tree in honor of creation; write a blessing for the occasion.

- ♻ Share this book with friends. Invite them to join you on your journey.

Over the long term, plan and put on a Stewardship of Creation service. Include hymns, songs, prayers, testimony, Scriptures, and sermons that highlight our special relationship to creation. Take up a special offering that can be used to purchase carbon offsets to neutralize your carbon footprint.

Follow Up

Form or join a Green Team in your church. Explore the terrain around your church. How might the Spirit be calling you to renew the earth around you? Share your findings with key leaders in your church, such as the pastor, trustees, the Christian education team, Sunday school or adult education team, and mission committee.

Notes

1. Repent

[1]*The New Interpreter's Bible*, Volume 1 (Abingdon Press, 1994); page 343.

[2]Scripture taken from the Holy Bible, NEW INTERNATIONAL VERSION.® Copyright ©1973, 1978, 1984 by International Bible Society. All rights reserved throughout the world. Used by permission of International Bible Society.

[3]"God's Earth Is Sacred: An Open Letter to Church and Society in the United States," The National Council of Churches (February 14, 2005).

[4]The US Census Bureau, *census.gov/ipc/www/popclockworld.html*.

[5]"World Population to Reach 9.1 Billion in 2050, UN Projects," UN News Centre (February 24, 2005).

[6]*Human Rights and the Ecological Imperative*, by Jim Swann, Whatcom Watch Online, chapter excerpt, *whatcomwatch.org/ php/WW_open.php?id=1036*.

[7]*The Consumer's Guide to Effective Environmental Choices: Practical Advice From the Union of Concerned Scientists*, by Michael Brower and Warren Leon (Three Rivers Press, 1999); page 44.

[8]The Species Alliance, *speciesalliance.org/about.php*.

[9]The Species Alliance.

[10]"Quarter of Mammals 'Face Extinction,'" by Corinne Podger, The British Broadcasting Company (May 21, 2002).

[11]"Honeybees Under Attack on All Fronts," by Debora MacKenzie, *New Scientist* (February 16, 2009).

[12]"Northeast Bat Die-Off Mirrors Honeybee Collapse," by Brian Mann, National Public Radio (February 19, 2008).

[13]"Ocean Warming's Effect on Phytoplankton," by Jane Kay, *The San Francisco Chronicle* (December 7, 2006).

[14]"Causes of Global Warming," EcoBridge, *ecobridge.org/ content/g_cse.htm*.

[15]"Findings of the IPCC Fourth Assessment Report: Climate Change Impacts," Union of Concerned Scientists (2007).

[16]*The Consumer's Guide to Effective Environmental Choices*; page 46.

[17]*Becoming the People of God: Caring for God's Earth*, edited by Richard J. Peck (Cokesbury, 2002); page 36.

[18]*The Consumer's Guide to Effective Environmental Choices*; page 46.

Notes

[19]"Ice Sheets," by Charles Bentley, Robert Thomas, and Isabella Velicogna, The United Nations Environment Programme.

[20]"Defiant Argentine Glacier Thrives Despite Warming," by Laura MacInnis, Planet Ark (February 4, 2009).

[21]"Indigenous Peoples at World Summit to Share Climate Change Observations, Experience, Traditional Coping Techniques," United Nations University (April 20, 2009).

[22]"Saving Florida's Vanishing Shores," The US Environmental Protection Agency (March 2002).

[23]"Global Temperatures Could Rise 6C by End of Century, Say Scientists," by Alok Jha, *The Guardian* (November 17, 2009).

[24]"Six Degrees Could Change the World," National Geographic Channel, *channel.nationalgeographic.com/episode/six-degrees-could-change-the-world-3188/Overview*.

[25]"Global Warming Visualized in 'Six Degrees,' " by Frazier Moore, *The Seattle Times* (February 10, 2008).

2. Reclaim

[1]Scripture quotations from THE MESSAGE. Copyright © by Eugene H. Peterson 1993, 1994, 1995, 1996, 2000, 2001, 2002. Used by permission of NavPress Publishing Group.

[2]"Islam and the Environment," by Hussein Amery, The International Development Research Center (February 16, 2006).

[3]*The New Interpreter's Bible*, page 346.

[4]"Climate Change," *Almanac of Policy Issues* (August 14, 2002).

[5]" 'High Confidence' That Planet Is Warmest in 400 Years," Nasa Earth Observatory (June 22, 2006).

[6]*Hot, Flat, and Crowded: Why We Need a Green Revolution—And How It Can Renew America*, by Thomas Friedman (Farrar, Straus, Giroux, 2008); page 133.

[7]*Hot, Flat, and Crowded*; page 133.

[8]"Tokyo Cherry Blossom Viewing Season Opens Early for Fourth Straight Year: Global Warming to Blame?" by Matthew McDermott, TreeHugger (May 23, 2009).

[9]"West Nile Virus Update—United States, January 1–August 19, 2008," Centers for Disease Control and Prevention.

[10]"Climate Change and Glaciers," National Park Service (June 2006).

[11]"Coral Bleaching—Will Global Warming Kill the Reefs?" Australian Academy of Science (April 2003) .

[12]"Global Warming," The Select Committee on Energy Independence and Global Warming, *globalwarming.house.gov*.

[13]"Millions of Missing Birds, Vanishing in Plain Sight," by Verlyn Klinkenborg, *The New York Times* (June 19, 2007).

[14]"Millions of Missing Birds."

[15]"Global Warming and Birds," Audubon, *audubon.org/globalWarming/ ImpactsBirdsWildlife.php.*

[16]From promotional material for *The End of the Line: Where Have All the Fish Gone?* at *nationalgeographic.com/endoftheline/.*

[17]"Still Waters, The Global Fish Crisis," by Fen Montaigne, *National Geographic* (April 2007).

[18]"Study: Only 10 Percent of Big Ocean Fish Remain," by Marsha Walton, CNN (May 15, 2003).

[19]"Carbon Dioxide Concentration," National Aeronautics and Space Administration, *climate.nasa.gov.*

[20]"Comment on 'Preindustrial to Modern Interdecadal Variability in Coral Reef pH,'" by Richard J. Matear and Ben I. McNeil, *Science Magazine*, Volume 314, Number 5799 (October 2006).

[21]"Cut CO_2 80% by 2020, not 2050," by Gerry Harrington, United Press International (August 3, 2009).

[22]"Still Waters."

[23]"Cod's Warning From Newfoundland," BBC News World Edition (December 16, 2002).

[24]From promotional material for *The End of the Line.*

[25]*MarineBio.org.*

[26]*The Free Dictionary, thefreedictionary.com/incandescent.*

[27]"The Future of Lighting: Scientists Create White Light That Is Eco-friendly, Affordable," by Sarah Bahari, *UNT Research* (Spring 2009).

[28]Boston CarbonPlus Calculator, *carboncalculator.growbostongreener.org/index.cfm?t=10.*

[29]*Strong's Greek Dictionary*, King James Version.

[30]*Last Child in the Woods: Saving Our Children From Nature-Deficit Disorder*, by Richard Louv (Algonquin Books of Chapel Hill, 2008); page 34.

[31]*Last Child in the Woods*; page 10.

[32]"Children and Nature 2008: A Report on the Movement to Reconnect Children to the Natural World," by Cheryl Charles, Richard Louv, Lee Bodner, and Bill Guns (January 2008), Children and Nature Network.

[33]"Children and Nature 2008."

3. Reduce

[1]*The Free Dictionary.*

[2]*The Free Dictionary.*

[3]There are three different versions of the Ten Commandments. The sabbath commandment is counted as the fourth commandment in the Jewish and Protestant traditions and as the third in the Catholic tradition.

Notes

[4]There was no New Testament in Jesus' day. His Bible was the Torah, what Christians call the Old Testament.

[5]See, for example, Mark 3:1-6 or Luke 13:10-17.

[6]In the Jewish calendar, in keeping with the rhythm of Creation in Genesis, each day begins the evening before. The Jewish sabbath begins at sundown on Friday night and concludes with the appearance of three stars in the night sky on Saturday evening.

[7]Seventh Day Adventists continue to recognize Saturday, the seventh day, as the sabbath. As their name implies, that is the day they gather for prayer and worship.

[8]*The Schocken Bible: Five Books of Moses: Genesis, Exodus, Leviticus, Numbers, Deuteronomy, A New Translation With Introduction, Commentary, and Notes*, Volume 1, by Everett Fox (Schocken Books, 1995); page 371.

[9]"DEQ Probes Sinclair Mishaps," by Dustin Bleizeffer in *The Casper Star-Tribune* (May 30, 2009).

[10]*Our Changing Planet: The View From Space*, by Michael D. King, Claire L. Parkinson, Kim C. Partington, and Robin G. Williams, editors (Cambridge University Press, 2007).

[11]*Our Changing Planet*; pages 74-77.

[12]*The Schocken Bible*; pages 385, 436.

[13]"Attack Asthma: Why America Needs a Public Health Defense to Battle Environmental Threats," *HealthyAmericans.org* (June 2000).

[14]"Give the Earth a Sabbath Day," by Christopher Ringwald, *The Christian Science Monitor* (September 12, 2007).

[15]"Rainy Days and Weekends," by Jessica Tanenbaum, ScienCentral, *sciencentral.com/articles/view.php3?article_id=218393094&cat=2_6* (April 2008).

[16]"Possible Pollution-Related 'Weekend Effect' in Lightning Behavior over the US," by T. L. Bell and D. Rosenfeld, *adsabs.harvard.edu/abs/2008AGUFM.A31J..05B* (December 2008).

[17]*The Schocken Bible*.

[18]*The New Interpreters Bible*; page 925.

[19]"How Can a Gallon of Gasoline Produce 20 Pounds of Carbon Dioxide?" *fueleconomy.gov/Feg/co2.shtml*.

[20]"What Is the Season of Creation?" *seasonofcreation.com/about/what*.

[21]Scripture taken from the New King James Version.® Copyright © 1982 by Thomas Nelson, Inc. Used by permission. All rights reserved.

4. Reuse

[1]*The United Methodist Hymnal* (The United Methodist Publishing House, 1989); 620.

[2]*The Faith We Sing* (Abingdon Press, 2000); 2059.

[3]"Why Building Community Is the Greenest Thing We Can Do," by Matt McDermott, Planet Green (June 15, 2009).

[4]For more information on the Christian Foundation for Children and Aging, go to *cfcausa.org*.

[5]"The World's Largest 'Landfill' Is in the Middle of the Ocean," by David Sokoll, EarthPortal, and "Afloat in the Ocean, Expanding Islands of Trash," by Lindsey Hoshaw, *The New York Times* (November 9, 2009).

[6]"The World's Largest 'Landfill' Is in the Middle of the Ocean."

[7]"Woman Tackles 'Great Garbage Patch,'" Ayesha Tejpar, CNN (October 29, 2009).

[8]"The Tragedy of the Commons," by Garrett Hardin, The Garrett Hardin Society, *garretthardinsociety.org/articles/art_tragedy_of_the_commons.html*.

[9]*Deep Economy: The Wealth of Communities and the Durable Future*, by Bill McKibben (Holt Paperbacks, 2007); page 42.

[10]"New Web-based Ecological Footprint Quiz Allows Individuals to Measure Their Impact on the Planet," Redefining Progress, *myfootprint.org*.

[11]Thanks to the Reverend Peter Sawtell of Eco-Justice Ministries for this helpful distinction.

[12]*Bowling Alone*, by Robert Putman (Simon and Schuster, 2000).

[13]"Junk Mail Impact," 41Pounds.org, *41pounds.org/impact/*.

[14]"An Exemplary Son in the Family of Saints," Greek Orthodox Metropolis of Toronto (Canada) Youth Department, *gocanada.org/youth/documents/saints/stbasil.pdf*.

[15]Soles4Soles, *soles4souls.org/about/history.html*.

[16]Voice of the Martyrs, *persecution.com*.

5. Recycle

[1]"Recycling," Inc.org, *inc.com/encyclopedia/recycling.html*.

[2]*Cradle to Cradle: Remaking the Way We Make Things*, by William McDonough and Michael Baungart (North Point Press, 2002).

[3]"Recycle Plastic Containers," SKS Bottle, *sks-bottle.com/Recycle_Plastic.html*.

[4]"Recycling Facts," Oberlin College, *oberlin.edu/recycle/facts.html*.

[5]"Church Recycling for the Whole Community," The National Partnership for the Environment, *nrpe.org/profiles/profiles_vi_C_27_01.htm*.

[6]"Amazing Homes and Offices Built From Shipping Containers," by Brian Clark Howard, *The Daily Green*, *thedailygreen.com/green-homes/latest/shipping-container-homes-460309*.

[7]"Recycling Facts."

[8]"Paper," WorldWatch Institute, *worldwatch.org/node/1497*.

[9]To learn more about TerraCycle, go to *terracycle.net/about_us*.

[10]"Church Deemed 'Greenest in America' by Audubon International," The National Religious Partnership for the Environment, *nrpe.org/profiles/profiles _vi_C_26_01.htm*.

[11]"Holy Redeemer Addition Goes Green: New Science and Media Center Exemplifies Caring for the Common Good," compiled by Ben Burnett, Oregon Interfaith Power and Light (2001).

[12]"Recycling Facts."

[13]"How Long Will Litter Last?" UrbanEdPartnership, *urbanedpartnership.org/ uclasp/issues/landfills/litter.html*.

[14]"Recycling Facts."

[15]To see a picture of the living roof at Arbroath Abbey, go to *greenroofs.com/ projects/pview.php?id=79*.

6. Rejoice!

[1]*Good Goats: Healing Our Image of God*, by Dennis Linn, Sheila Fabricant Linn, and Matthew Linn (Paulist Press, 1994); page 11.

[2]Strong's Greek Dictionary, *strongsnumbers.com/greek/2889.htm*.

[3]Quote at *thinkexist.com*.

[4]*Surprised by Hope: Rethinking Heaven, the Resurrection, and the Mission of the Church*, by N. T. Wright (HarperOne, 2008); page 193.

[5]*Surprised by Hope*; page 148.

[6]"Eyes Turned Skyward Looking Back at Earth," SpaceQuotations, *spacequotations.com/earth.html*.

[7]"Eyes Turned Skyward Looking Back at Earth."

[8]CarbonDescent, *carbondescent.org.uk/glossary.php*.

[9]"Low Carbon Diet Personal CO_2 Calculator," *empowermentinstitute.net/lcd/ lcd_files/LCDcalcNet.html*.

[10]*An Inconvenient Truth*, by Al Gore (Rodale, 2006); page 12.

[11]"Eyes Turned Skyward Looking Back at Earth."

[12]"Heaven Is Green: An Interview With Wangari Maathai," by Mia MacDonald (May 16, 2005), The Green Belt Movement.

[13]"Faith in Action Report: Communities of Faith Bringing Hope for the Planet," The Sierra Club (June 2008).

[14]"Bottled Water Isn't Healthier Than Tap, Report Reveals," by James Owen, *National Geographic* News (February 24, 2006).

[15]"Faith in Action Report."

Rebekah Simon-Peter, an ordained United Methodist pastor with a degree in environmental studies, worked as an acid-rain researcher and volunteer naturalist before receiving her call to ministry. After more than a decade of pastoring churches, she is now a sought-after presenter, sharing the "green" gospel with churches, interfaith groups, and community groups. She lives in Rawlins, Wyoming, where she is the director of BridgeWorks, a ministry that specializes in building bridges of understanding.